The London 1948 Olym|

A Collectors' Guide

Bob Wilcock

Society of Olympic Collectors

2012

Published in Great Britain 2012

by

The Society of Olympic Collectors

24, Hamilton Crescent, Brentwood, Essex, CM14 5ES

© The Society of Olympic Collectors
the Author and Contributors
2012

ISBN 978-0-9558236-1-9

Printed by
Warners Midlands plc
The Maltings, Manor Lane, Bourne, Lincolnshire, PE10 9PH

The London 1948 Olympic Games

A Collectors' Guide

Contents

Foreword

This is a book for collectors and would-be collectors of the stamps and postal history of the London 1948 Olympic Games, and shows how, through collections, the story of an Olympic Games can be told and recalled, how memories can be preserved.

Collectors of British stamps and postal history will find as much to interest them as will Olympic collectors. The story of the 1948 Olympic stamp issue was told in full detail by Douglas Muir in the *Philatelic Bulletin* in 1989. His exposé cannot be bettered, and I am grateful to him, the British Postal Museum & Archive, and Royal Mail for permission to reproduce the article in full. A small amount of information has been added, but more significantly, all the artists designs held by BPMA are now reproduced together for the first time, together with artwork from two of the artists.

W. G. Stitt Dibden's 1959 publication "*The 1948 Olympics at Wembley*" was an invaluable source for the postal history, supplemented by information in the Official Report "*XIV Olympiad London 1948*", the unique *Postmaster's Record* in a private collection, and examination and study of hundreds of covers, cards and other items posted during the Games and relating to them. The latter in particular has led to some new discoveries, revealed for the first time in this book.

In putting together the chapter on stamps commemorating 1948 Olympians and medal winners, I was helped considerably by Sports Philatelists International's "*Olympians on Stamps*" and the works of Alvaro Trucchi published by UICOS in Italy. These works have been consolidated, and updated, and for the first time, all the stamps and postal items are illustrated in colour. It took time, but it proved neither difficult nor expensive to find and buy every single item illustrated in these chapters.

Stamps and postcards are comprehensively covered, but the coverage of ephemera and collectors cards, while detailed, is no more than representative, to provide a guide to the fascinating material available to be collected. As always, it is for the individual to decide what and how to collect, and which aspects of the 1948 Olympic story to concentrate on. No two collections will be the same, but that is the beauty of it, and I shall be pleased if this book is not just a work of reference, but a source of inspiration.

I must add my gratitude to Alan Sabey for enabling me to copy and include many items from his medal-winning collection, and the many other collectors who have provided me with information, and loaned me items in their collections to be copied for inclusion in the book; it would have been a poorer work without their willing help, as it would without the unfailing help and support of my wife Ruth. I wish to record my thanks to her and to everybody who has assisted me.

Bob Wilcock
June 2012

THE GAMES OF THE XIVTH OLYMPIAD
LONDON 1948

Edström, 1942-1952

PALAU   80¢

In June 1939, just before the start of the Second World War, the International Olympic Committee awarded the Games of the XIIIth Olympiad, 1944, to London. The war meant that those Games were never held. The war finished in May 1945 and by October 1945 the British Olympic Council were in discussion with the President of the IOC, Sigfrid Edström of Sweden, about the possibility of London hosting the Games of the 14th Olympiad in 1948. A formal bid followed and in March 1946 a postal vote by IOC members resulted in the award of the Games to London.

As in 1908, London had just two years to prepare for the Games. Unlike in 1908, at least the stadium was ready, Wembley Stadium, built in 1923 for the 1924 Empire Exhibition.

Lord Burghley

In July 1947 the Postmaster General authorised the issue of two stamps and in August 1947 invitations to submit stamp designs were issued to twenty artists and printers. One of those designs proved controversial.

At the Antwerp Olympics in 1928 David Cecil, Lord Burghley won Gold in the 400 metres hurdles. In 1933 he became a member of the International Olympic Committee, and in 1936 Chairman of the British Olympic Association. From 1946 he was Chairman of the Organising Committee for the 1948 Olympic Games.

One of the artists, G.T. Knipe, working for the printers Harrison & Sons Ltd, was inspired to include two hurdlers in his design, one of those hurdlers being Lord Burghley. He anonymised the image, removing the number '10' from the jersey, modifying the face to make it unrecognisable, and darkening the hair, but the fact that the image was based on a photograph caused considerable concern. The photograph was owned by Reuters and the Post Office were worried about copyright. It was felt that Lord Burghley's permission would be needed, but the real worry was "that it would hardly be proper to depict one of his Majesty's subjects on a postage stamp bearing the King's effigy". Nonetheless Knipe's design was one of the six chosen to be submitted to the King; four were recommended, Knipe's was one of two reserve designs so that the King had a choice. The King however followed the recommendations, and did not choose Knipe's design. The delicate problem was therefore avoided. Olympic collectors had to wait until 1957 for a stamp depicting Lord Burghley, issued by the Dominican Republic as one of a set commemorating Olympic medallists.

In the following chapter, Douglas Muir, Curator British Postal Museum and Archive, sets out the full story of the British stamp issue.

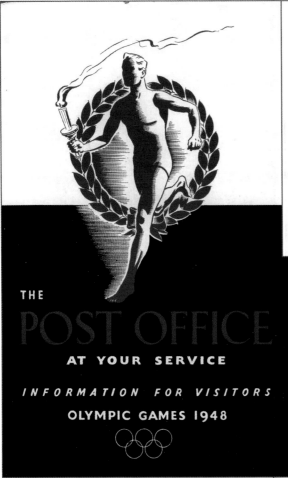

WELCOME !

Front cover and brief extracts from a 20 page booklet issued by the Post Office, principally giving postage rates in Great Britain and to overseas

To the many visitors who have come from Overseas to Wembley the British Post Office extends a cordial welcome and has pleasure in offering the services of its various departments.

Brief particulars of these services are given in this booklet.

Postal, Telephone and Telegraph Facilities for the XIVth Olympiad

There will be a Post Office in the Wembley Stadium grounds for the transaction of all classes of post office business and a special postmark will be put on letters posted in certain marked boxes in the grounds.

Special commemorative stamps $2\frac{1}{2}$d., 3d, 6d. and 1s. will be on sale at all Post Offices. (Commemorative stamps have been issued in Great Britain on only eight previous occasions since the world's first postage stamp was issued in this country in 1840.) Special commemorative Air Letter forms will also be available at the price of 6d. each.

A new telephone exchange—aptly named Corinthian—has been installed at Wembley, and there will be a telephone network within the Stadium for intercommunication between officials conducting the Games. Many call offices will be provided for visitors.

Teleprinter communication will link Wembley and other centres where Games are held.

The 1948 Olympic Games Issue

Douglas N Muir (Curator Philately, British Postal Museum & Archive)

After the end of World War II a number of requests were received by the GPO [General Post Office] for special stamp issues marking various events which took place in fairly rapid succession. There was the Victory itself, pressure for a regional issue for the Channel Islands (which eventually resulted in the Liberation pair of stamps) and various royal events such as the Silver Wedding of King George VI and Queen Elizabeth, the marriage of Princess Elizabeth, and the birth of Prince Charles. As the stamp issuing policy at the time was very conservative, not all serious proposals resulted in commemorative stamps, but one event could not be ignored, and that was the holding of the Games of the 14th Olympiad in London and the south of England.

First discussions within the GPO took place in May 1947, and on 28th July of that year the Postmaster General authorised the issue of two values – 2½d and 3d. This was the current standard, as in the Victory and Channel Islands Liberation issues, though the number of values was later increased to four. The Council of Industrial Design was asked to submit a list of possible artists, and they nominated 10. The Post Office then added a further 10, including four printers, the College of Arms, and previously successful artists such as Edmund Dulac, Harold Nelson and Barnett Freedman. Not all took up the challenge, and only 13 of the 20 submitted designs. A total of 26 designs were received. All of these are now in the British Postal Museum & Archive (BPMA).

The instructions to the artists were detailed, and make interesting reading:

"To celebrate the occasion of the Olympic Games to be held in this country in 1948 it is proposed to issue commemorative postage stamps of the 2½d and 3d denominations.

The stamps will be approximately the same colour as the current stamps of the relative values except that the dye used will be of a richer and deeper shade than in the current issues of the values named. They will be printed by the photogravure process. ... The denomination must appear once or twice in clear numerals approximately the size of the numerals in the

current 2½d and 3d stamps. The denomination of the stamp may not be shown in words. The legend 'Olympic Games 1948' must also appear. No other words, letters or numerals may be introduced .

The design must include space for a representation of the King's head (of not less than the size in the current 2½d stamp) which may be on the right, left, or central. It is suggested that a position to the right or left will give greater scope for the associated design. The Head may be shown uncrowned but if so a crown proportionate to the size of the Head must be included in the design. The actual representation of the head (of the size to suit the design) will be provided by the Post Office separately. The artist's drawing should include merely a rough indication of the head in the space which it will fill.

The remaining space should be devoted to a design suitable to the occasion of the Olympic Games preferably symbolising athletes generally and the International character of the gathering.

The photogravure process by which the stamps are to be printed reproduces a number of gradated tones, and care should be taken to use material that will permit of photographing each tone in its true value. A card showing the range of tones is enclosed, and the finished drawing should be as nearly as possible in the same colour, a kind of sepia-grey. The details embodied in the design should be such as can be reproduced in the size of the finished stamp. It is essential that any designs submitted should be suitable for immediate reproduction, and to this end it is hoped that you will maintain, from an early stage, the closest touch with the stamp printers. ...

The dimensions of the drawing should preferably, though not necessarily, be six times the actual size, i.e. 5.16 ins. by 9.06 ins., and it would be of great assistance if a photograph of it of approximately stamp size could be submitted with each drawing. ..."

The designs had to be submitted by 22 October and would become the property of the Postmaster General. A fee of 40 guineas would be paid for one or more designs for each denomination with a further fee of

160 guineas for any design accepted for use. A note at the end explained the reason for the King's head:

"The International Postal Union Convention provides that postage stamps should bear an indication of the Country of issue in Roman characters. This has never been done in the case of British stamps. It has been held that the Sovereign's Head is so well known that other countries can be expected to recognise it. Britain invented the postage stamp and it is no doubt for this reason that no other Country has raised the matter officially. This is why the King's Head must be given a prominent position on any British postage stamp."

In the files it is noted that 25 designs were received though, in fact, 26 are now in the BPMA. The one designer not mentioned in the lists is G. Knipe, though he worked for Harrisons and the clerks may have considered that two of Harrisons' other submissions were so similar as to be counted as one. The only difference was in the legend which appeared in Esperanto in one and English in the other.

The artists who submitted designs were:

Leonard Beaumont   (4)
Harold Nelson   (2)
Wilson Parker   (3)
John Armstrong   (2)
The College of Arms (George Bellew)(2)
Percy Metcalfe   (1)
John Farleigh   (1)
Edmund Dulac   (1)
Thomas Eckersley   (1)
Abram Games   (1)
   (often misrepresented in the files as 'Abraham')
Reynolds Stone   (1)
Bradbury Wilkinson (W.S. Matthews and
   A.C. King)   (2)
Harrisons (including G. Knipe)   (3)
Waterlows (S.D. Scott) (1)

At the end of October representatives of the Royal Fine Arts Commission for Scotland and the Council of Industrial Design were invited to view the designs and make their recommendations.

Those from the Royal Fine Arts Commission for Scotland (Haswell Miller, Pilkington Jackson and

The two designs submitted by John Armstrong. The lower design was preferred by the Royal Fine Arts Commission for Scotland and was essayed for submission to the King but was not recommended.

The two designs submitted by George Bellew. The lower design includes the Wembley Lion sculptures.

The four designs submitted by Leonard Beaumont. All include the Olympic Rings, and three have a stylised Greek head

Reginald Fairlie) looked at the designs in Postal Headquarters on 30 October and chose five (in order):

No. 21 – Armstrong's design with mounted horse
No. 14 – Dulac's
No. 10 – Metcalfe's
No. 7 – Harold Nelson's heraldic design
No. 9 – Waterlow's (Scott)

No. 21 by Armstrong was regarded as distinctly the best design. The others were about equal, though that by Scott was placed last.

The following day the representatives of the Council of Industrial Design arrived. They were Sir Kenneth Clark, Sir Francis Meynell, and Mrs Tomrley, the Secretary. Their choice was similar, but different in details, and was largely to be followed by the GPO:

A   No. 15 – Knipe of Harrisons – for 2½d
B   No. 23 – Games – for 3d
C   No. 9 – Waterlows – for 6d
D   No. 14 – Dulac – for 1s
E   No. 10 – Metcalfe

At discussions with the Director General of the Post Office and subsequently the Postmaster General on 4 November the designs were chosen for submission to the King. These were No. 15 (Knipe), or No. 10 (Metcalfe) for the 2½d stamp, No. 23 (Games) for the 3d stamp, No. 9 Scott for the 6d stamp, and No. 14 (Dulac) for the 1s stamp.

If No. 10 were to be chosen for the 2½d value, as indeed it was, consideration should be given to replacing the five hands by the five continents, the letter 'M' in both 'Olympic' and 'Games' to be reshaped. This was in fact done on the first essay, the five continents referring to the Olympic Rings.

For the Abram Games design used on the 3d value the artist was to be asked to bring out the face and the indications of speed, though this was not ready in time for the first essay. The Scott design (No. 9) was particularly chosen for the 6d stamp because it was felt that it should be relatively simple to cut a letterpress die for use on the air mail letter form which it was also intended to issue.

Torch Runner design by Reynolds Stone (with his signature superimposed)

The Postmaster General thought that the King's choice would be too restricted with only five designs, and he personally liked No. 21 – Armstrong's design, also thought highly of by the Royal Fine Art Commission for Scotland. So these six designs were sent to Harrisons for bromides and essays to be prepared. The printers were told to make sure that the features of the jumper on design No. 15 could not be recognised.

All agreed that Harold Nelson's heraldic design (chosen by the Scottish Fine Art Commission) was 'not in the running'.

There was now a pause in activity (in the files at least)

until February 1948. Christmas intervened and Harrisons were also working on the Silver Wedding and Channel Islands Liberation issues. However essays of the six designs were to hand by 18 February, and the Postmaster General (the Rt. Hon. Wilfred Paling MP) asked for an audience with the King to seek his approval. This was granted on 26 February and the essays were shown in the colours of the recommended values – i.e. blue for the 2½d even though the value still read 3d. The essays were numbered A to F with essays E and F (the designs by Armstrong and Knipe) not being recommended but still essayed in the colour of the 2½d.

Design submitted by Thomas Eckersley

John Farleigh's submission

*The submitted design by Abram Games F.S.I.A. (right).
This was selected by the Council for Industrial Design
but the Post Office asked that the artist bring out the
face and the indications of speed. This was done
(above) and the lettering and crown were made bolder.*

*Submitted artwork by
Percy Metcalfe (right).
Originally this drawing was
as the bromide (above),
with the value of 3^D, a
different crown, and hands
beneath the globe. The
hands were changed to
rings, and an essay was
accepted by the King on
March 1^{sr} 1948. Value and
crown were changes, and
also the two letters "M".
The artwork was then
meticulously painted over.*

Abram Games—Artist's drawings

The germ of an idea—including a Torch, and the first attempt to work in the lettering: the Olympic rings are causing difficulty—only 3 are shown.

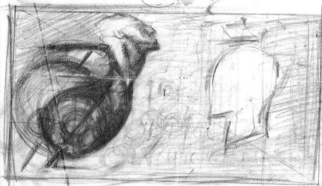

As the design takes shape the torch metamorphoses into a head.

The turning point—the head is moved to the left

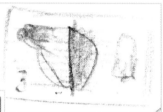

The key drawing showing the design close to realisation (see p. 7).

A sketch drawn by A. Games to explain the construction of the design to C. P. Rang (Editor of *Gibbons Stamp Monthly*) in October 1948.

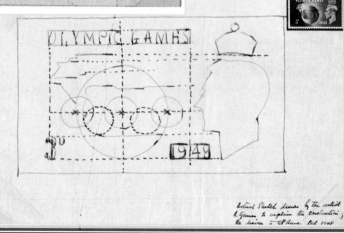

Harold Nelson

Below, the letter inviting submissions.

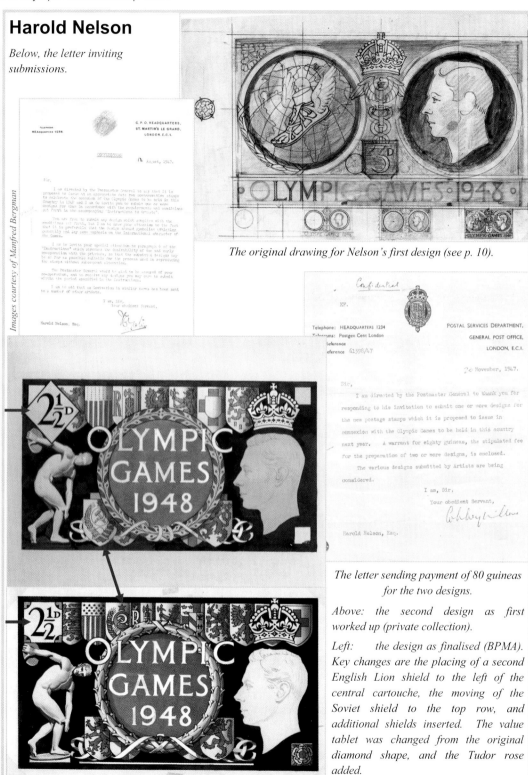

The original drawing for Nelson's first design (see p. 10).

(see p. 10)

The letter sending payment of 80 guineas for the two designs.

Above: the second design as first worked up (private collection).

Left: the design as finalised (BPMA). Key changes are the placing of a second English Lion shield to the left of the central cartouche, the moving of the Soviet shield to the top row, and additional shields inserted. The value tablet was changed from the original diamond shape, and the Tudor rose added.

Submitted design by Edmund Dulac (signed) showing "a running Victory calling to the nations of the world".
Selected by both the Royal Fine Art Commission for Scotland and the Council of Industrial Design,
it was chosen for the 1/- value.

Bromide of the original design by Stanley D. Scott of
Waterlows (above) and original artwork (below),
altered to show the decided value of 6^D

The two designs submitted by Harold Nelson

Design submitted by A.C. King (left) and W.S. Matthews of Bradbury Wilkinson & Co

The three designs submitted by Wilson Parker

The three designs submitted by Harrison, the middle design having text in Esperanto

The recommendations were:

> Essay A (Artist P. Metcalfe) is recommended for the 2½d stamp
>
> Essay B (Artist A. Games) is recommended for the 3d stamp
>
> Essay C (Artist Scott [Waterlows]) is recommended for the 6d stamp
>
> Essay D (Artist E. Dulac) is recommended for the 1s stamp

The King retained the essays for a day or two for proper examination and then returned them, approved, but with comments in his own hand. On Essay A he wrote 'Change the Crown to be the same as in B' and on Essay B ' This is the right crown'. The final essays showed the changes as required.

Contact was now made with the artists for them to carry out the requisite changes and to insert the correct denominations. Games submitted new artwork strengthening the lines indicating speed, but the other artists reworked the original pieces of artwork. If the design by Metcalfe is examined minutely, traces of its original denomination (3d) can be seen coming through the background colour but none of the other changes is visible. Final essays were approved in May.

The stamps were issued on 29 July 1948, the first day of the Games, and the Post Office sent out a press release giving some background details:

"The 2½d stamp, designed by Mr Percy Metcalfe, C.V.O., R.D.I., shows the globe, symbolising the universality of the Games, surrounded by the laurel wreath of Victory.

The 3d stamp, designed by Mr Abram Games, F.S.I.A., shows the figure of an athlete combined with the world, symbolising the athletic striving of all the nations taking part in the Games. The horizontal drawing of the athlete and the lines running from him express the movement and vitality of the Games.

The 6d stamp, designed by Mr Stanley D. Scott of Waterlow and Sons Ltd., shows the King's head superimposed on the five interlaced rings. Formalised laurel branches on the left and right, each with 14 leaves, are indicative of the Fourteenth Olympiad.

The 1s stamp, designed by Mr Edmund Dulac, shows a winged Victory running round the world calling to the nations and holding out the crown of laurel destined for the victor in the Games.

All four stamps have been produced by Messrs Harrison and Sons Ltd., of London, Hayes (Middlesex) and High Wycombe (Bucks) by the photogravure process. They have been printed on paper especially provided for the purpose by Messrs. Portals (John Allen & Sons) Ltd. at their Ivybridge Mills. The air letter forms (but not the stamp printed on them) have been printed by Messrs McCorquodales of Wolverton (Bucks). Messrs Harrison and Sons Ltd. printed the stamp on these forms by the photogravure process.!

Biographical details were then given of the artists:

*"**Percy Metcalfe, C.V.O., R.D.I.** has had a long artistic career. He is on the Livery of the Goldsmiths' Company, has designed coinage for Eire, Turkey, Egypt, Iraq, New Zealand, Fiji, Greece, and Bulgaria, the Great Seal of the Realm, 1928, the Great Seals of Eire and South Africa; Coronation medals.*

***Abram Games, F.S.I.A.,** born in London, age 34, is self-taught; worked in studio until 21, then free lance. Joined the Army in 1940 and made War Office poster designer, designing exclusively for the Army, including the controversial 'A.T.S. Glamour Girl'. War posters exhibited in London, New York, Paris, Moscow, Leningrad, Prague, Switzerland, etc. One man shows in Stockholm (1943) and Brussels (1946). Demobilised 1946 and free lance once again. Lecturer in design at Royal College of Art, London.*

***Stanley D. Scott,** age 28, designer for Messrs Waterlow & Sons Ltd. Received art training at the West Ham School of Art and joined the firm in 1935. Saw six years' war service with the Field Survey, Royal Engineers, almost four of which were spent overseas with the Eighth Army.*

***Edmund Dulac,** well-known in the artistic world. His work includes book illustrations, portraits, caricatures, stage settings and costumes and decorations. He designed and modelled King's Poetry Prize medal; the King George VI Coronation stamp (1937), the King George VI cameo portrait used in all*

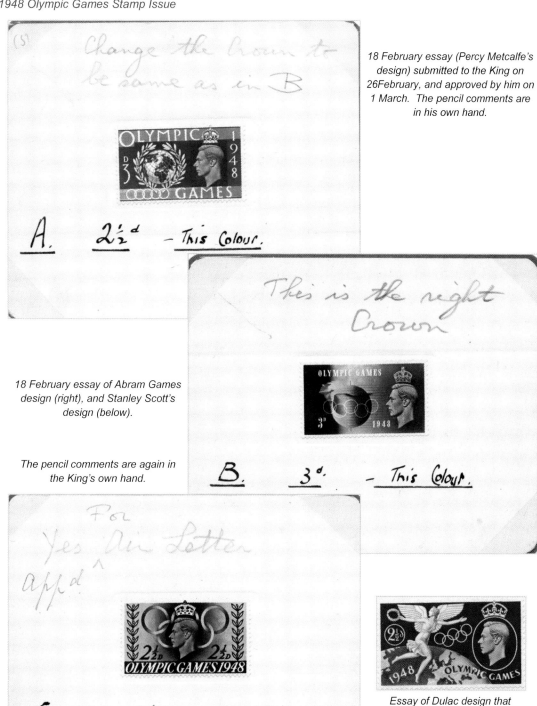

18 February essay (Percy Metcalfe's design) submitted to the King on 26 February, and approved by him on 1 March. The pencil comments are in his own hand.

18 February essay of Abram Games design (right), and Stanley Scott's design (below).

The pencil comments are again in the King's own hand.

Essay of Dulac design that was approved for 1/- value

the current stamps. He also designed the present 7d to 5s stamps. *The Free French Colonial stamps and banknotes and the first post-war stamp for Metropolitan France – "Marianne" – were also designed by Mr Dulac."*

The stamps were to be printed *"on the special Titanium paper already supplied"*, the 6d stamp in non-fugitive ink. Preparations for printing continued over the months from May through to July.

On 27 May discussions took place about how many stamps should be printed. The quantities were considered in the light of sales of the Silver Wedding and Channel Islands stamps. In the case of the 2½d Silver Wedding stamp one million sheets had proved to be too few. For the 3d, 6d and 1s values, the Director of Postal Services considered that 100,000 sheets (12 million sets) should be provided for philatelic sales. As a result the revised quantities of stamps were as follows:

2½d   1,250,000 sheets of 120
       (150,000,000 stamps)
3d   250,000 sheets (30,000,000 stamps)
6d   200,000 sheets (24,000,000 stamps)
1s   250,000 sheets (30,000,000 stamps)

This was an increase for the 2½d and 1s values but, in fact, the final quantities ordered from the printers were even higher. As reported on 28 January 1949 they were:

2½d   1,375,000 sheets (165,000,000 stamps)
3d   300,000 sheets (36,000,000 stamps)
6d   240,000 sheets (28,800,000 stamps)
1s   300,000 sheets (36,000,000 stamps)

This does, however, conceal considerable over-ordering by those concerned. On 3 September a memo stated that *"it seems quite clear that our guess regarding the demand for the 3d, 6d and 1s stamps was wide of the mark. ... the only way to dispose of these stamps is for the Stores to keep on pumping them out, holding back the normal 3d, 6d and 1s stamps until the Olympic Games are disposed of."* At that point there were still outstanding:

2½d   67,000 sheets
3d   120,000 sheets
6d   95,000 sheets
1s   166,000 sheets

In other words about half the printing of the higher values remained. Stocks were not finally recalled until the end of January 1949, and the print figures for the UPU issue which appeared on 10 October were considerably reduced.

As can be seen from the detailed figures, an additional 13,200 sheets (1,584,000 stamps) of each value were taken for overprinting, for use in British postal agencies. This was a vast reduction from the 82,500 sheets originally envisaged, done *"in the light of the experience gained with the Royal Silver Wedding overprints"*. The postal agencies needing these were in Tangier (3,300 sheets), Tetuan (3,300 sheets), Bahrain (2,200 sheets), Kuwait (2,200 sheets), and Muscat and Dubai (2,200 sheets). Even these estimates were wide of the mark as final sales figures were much lower, as shown in the table. It can be seen that only about a quarter of the print figures were actually sold and, of course, a good number of these went to stamp dealers.

The Postmaster General was asked on 23 February 1949 about sales figures. These he gave to the nearest thousand. He regretted that information regarding stamps bought by philatelists was not available: *"The Post Office has no means of identifying postage stamps bought for philatelic purposes as opposed to those bought for use for prepayment of postage."*

Approval of Essays & Proofs			
	Essay Approved	*Cyl. Proof approved*	*1st supply received*
2½d	27 May	22 June	29 June
3d	24 May	14 June	21 June
6d	6 May	16 July	17 July
1s	27 May	1 July	13 July
Air letter		11 May	

References

British Postal Museum and Archive files:
Post 102/12 (M133488/49) Postage Stamps Commemorative: Channel Islands Liberation and Olympic Games.
Post 52/1002 Unified Stamps – Olympic Games, issue and airletter.

The Issued Stamps

Value	Postal purpose	Designer	Number sold (approx)*	Cylinders#
2½ d	Letter rate	Percy Metcalfe	155,350,000	2I, 2B, 2.I; 3I, 3B, 3.I, 3.B
3 d	Registration Fee	Abram Games	32,554,000	1I, 1.I
6 d	Air mail letter	Stanley D. Scott	24,397,000	9I, 9.I
1/-	Overseas & parcels	Edmund Dulac	32,187,000	3I, 3.I, 3.B

* Numbers exclude stamps overprinted for use in the British Post Offices in Bahrain, Kuwait, Muscat, Morocco Agencies and Tangier (see p. 4)	# 'I' indicates bottom margin imperf, top margin perf; 'B' indicates both margins perforated

A detailed breakdown gave figures for wastage etc. and final sales

	2½ d	3 d	6 d	1/-
Ordered	165,000,000	36,000,000	28,800,000	36,000,000
Good	156,965,880	34,311,240	26,278,560	34,638,000
Waste	8,034,120	1,688,760	2,521,440	1,362,000
Transferred for over-printing	1,584,000	1,584,000	1,584,000	1,584,000
Specimens etc	2,425	2,425	2,545	2,425
Departmental waste etc	1,955	1,355	1,595	1,235
Issued to Postmasters	155,377,500	32,723,460	24,690,420	33,050,340
Withdrawn from sale January 1949	26,520	168,818	293,050	862,875
Postmasters' estimated sales*	155,350,980	32,554,642	24,397,370	32,187,465

* Sales were probably a little lower, because postmasters were still returning stamps when the list was compiled.

Sales in the Postal Agencies

Value	Bahrain	Kuwait	Muscat	Morocco Agencies	Tangier
2 ½ d	99,304	89,264	73,998	107,309	101,965
3 d	112,515	91,203	72,226	100,020	101,638
6 d	112,919	83,677	68,904	94,278	101,175
1/-	87,858	83,395	66,867	93,304	96,190

Cylinders

Value	Bahrain	Kuwait	Muscat	Morocco Agencies	Tangier
2 ½ d	2.I	2I	2.I	2I	2I, 2.I
3 d	1.I	1.I	1I	1I	1I, 1.I
6 d	9I	9.I	9I	9I	9.I
1/-	3I	3I	3.I	3I	3.I

Chronology of the 1948 Olympic Games Issue

May 1947	First discussions
28 July 1947	PMG authorises issue of two values ($2^{1}/_{2}$d and 3d)
8 August 1947	Council of Industrial Design suggest artists
12 August 1947	Letter to artists inviting submission of designs in accordance with instructions given
22 October 1947	All designs to be received by this date
30 October 1947	Scottish Fine Arts Commission view designs at GPO Headquarters
31 October 1947	Council of Industrial Design view designs
4 November 1947	Designs chosen to submit to the King. Harrisons to produce bromides and essays of six designs
10 December 1947	Question in Parliament: in reply the PMG announced the issue of the four Olympic stamps
18 February 1948	Essays to hand
26 February 1948	PMG sees the King. Six essays shown A-F, E and F not being recommended
27 February 1948	The King returns essays, approving C and D
1 March 1948	The King has approved A, B, C, D, with the crown to be changed on A
3 March 1948	Conference at GPO Headquarters—changes in detail. "Further colour pulls wanted when denominations are altered". Essays returned to Harrisons.
8 March 1948	Discussions at Royal Mint on airletter
15 March 1948	Printers agree that the airletter should be printed letterpress by McCorquodales with the stamp gravure by Harrisons
19 March 1948	New drawing by Games showing 3d inserted with more graded shading handed over to Harrisons
4 May 1948	Essay of 3d value approved
6 May 1948	Essay of 6d value approved
11 May 1948	Cylinder proof of 6d value for airletter approved
27 May 1948	Essays of $2^{1}/_{2}$d and 1s values approved
29 July 1948	First day of sale of the stamps and airletter, and first day of the Games.

P.A.-Reuter Photo

Black and white photograph of the stamps, on glossy photo paper, with duplicated press release pasted on the reverse (stamp images 91 x 51mm, photograph 205 x 152mm; reproduced @ 70% actual size); press cutting

Special postage stamps which have been made to commemorate the Olympic Games. The issue is in four denominations, 2½d., 3d., 6d. and 1s. In addition there will be an air letter form with a replica of the 6d. stamp. The stamps are available at all post offices today, the official opening day of the Games.

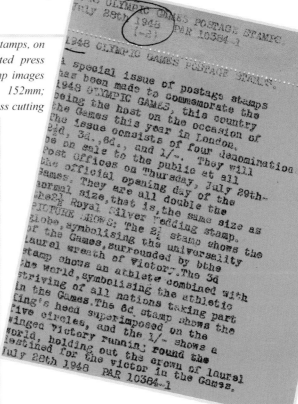

1948 OLYMPIC GAMES POSTAGE STAMPS.
July 28th 1948 PAR 10384-1
(-2)

1948 OLYMPIC GAMES POSTAGE STAMPS.

A special issue of postage stamps has been made to commemorate the 1948 OLYMPIC GAMES, this country being the host on the occasion of the Games this year in London. The issue consists of four denomination 2½d, 3d.,6d., and 1/-. They will be on sale to the public at all Post Offices on Thursday, July 29th- the official opening day of the Games. They are all double the normal size,that is,the same size as the Royal Silver Wedding stamp.

PICTURE SHOWS: The 2½ stamp shows the Globe, symbolising the universality of the Games,surrounded by the Laurel wreath of Victory.The 3d stamp shows an athlete combined with the world, symbolising the athletic striving of all nations taking part in the Games.The 6d stamp shows the King's head superimposed on the five circles, and the 1/- shows a winged Victory running round the world, holding out the crown of laurel destined for the victor in the Games.
July 28th 1948 PAR 10384-1

Air letter

From the outset, it had been planned to issue a commemorative air letter, the first such ever. At the time, air letters were printed letterpress by McCorquodales, with a special letterpress for the imprinted stamp. As has been mentioned, the 6d design, the value needed for the air letter, was specifically recommended as being suitable for letterpress reproduction, but there was always some doubt about this. Discussions took place between the Post Office, the Royal mint, and the printers at the beginning of March 1948.

On 8 March the Royal Mint was shown an essay of the 6d value and asked if they could supply 12 or 16 rotary letterpress dies for delivery to McCorquodales by the end of May. For the Mint, Mr Whittaker said that "*this could be done if an existing engraving of the King's head could be used, but that it would be impossible if a new engraving of the head was required.*" The head used for the current air letter would be right for size, but the engraver would need a line drawing as well.

Harrisons had offered to print the stamp in photogravure if letterpress should prove impracticable, and it was agreed that this was "*likely to produce a much better job whilst obviating the necessity for converting a photogravure design into letterpress, with the risk of losing the effect.*" Difficulties of registration were cited by Harrisons as a reason for them printing the whole job in gravure, but it was decided that the background stipple and text would be printed in letterpress by McCorquodales at their works at Wolverton, and the sheets would then be sent to High Wycombe for the stamp to be added in gravure by Harrisons.

Warrants for 4,200,000 forms, including stamped waste, were issued, being a month's supply, but, not unnaturally, problems arose in production. McCorquodales had recently rejected 30 tons of paper for air letter production as being of poor quality. The replacement delivery was of better quality but in a drab shade rather than azure, and was rejected as far as the Olympic issue was concerned. Because of the paper quota system, however, it was accepted for use on ordinary air letters. Up to standard supplies were purchased from another firm.

Printing took place on the same rotary press used by McCorquodales for postal orders.

About half the amount had been printed by McCorquodales, and supplied to Harrisons by May, when the latter asked that no more be sent for the time being. This was because the cylinder was not approved until 11 May, and no printing was taking place. When the stamps had been printed on the uncut sheets, these were returned to McCorquodales, for cutting and gumming.

The air letter was placed on sale on 29 July, the same day as the stamps. Total sales amounted to some 4,060,000.

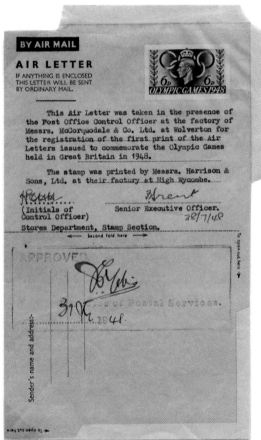

Registration copy of the air letter.

Douglas Muir's article on the stamps and air letter was first published in the Philatelic Bulletin February, March and April 1989. It is reproduced with a small amount of additional information from BPMA archives, and with additional illustrations.

A pair of uncut air letter sheets, being positions 7 & 8 being one of four pairs from a sheet of 8 air letters.
It is a duplicate of a sheet approved by the Director of Postal Services on 11 May 1948.

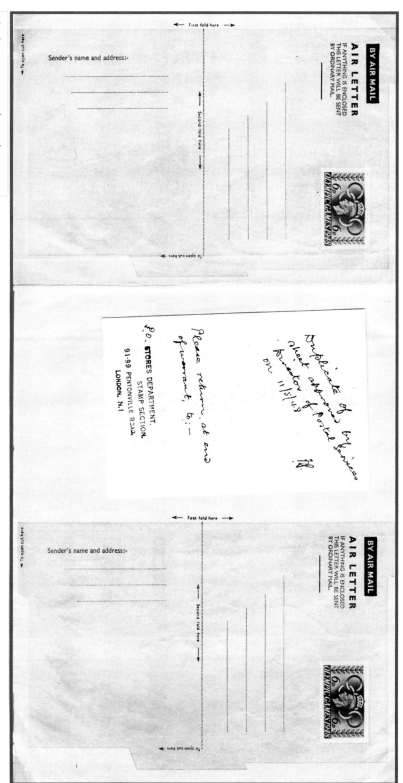

Private collection

The Overseas Territories Overprints

Bahrain

Muscat

Kuwait

Morocco Agencies

Tangier

First Day Covers

Bahrain

Kuwait

Morocco Agencies

Muscat

It is reported that there are no FDCs for Muscat. Whether this is because the stamps did not arrive is not clear. Philatelic covers were sent later.

Muscat stamps are also known used in Bahrain.

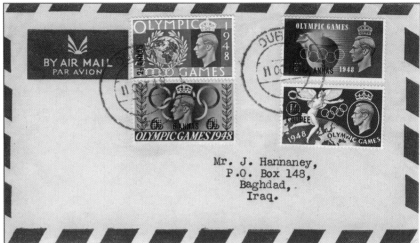

Tangier

A mystery cover (below) has un-overprinted stamps. It is understandable for a sheet of one value to slip through, but all 4 values is a puzzle!

Postmark from a non registered cover

Tristan da Cunha

Tristan da Cunha, in the South Atlantic, used British stamps until 1961. Covers with Olympic stamps are known, but rare (as is any mail from the Island).

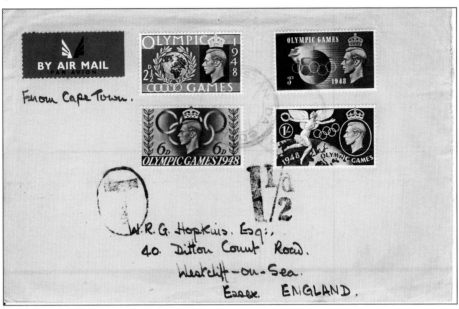

The Tristan da Cunha circular cancel is undated (it was introduced on 2 February 1948). It is not clear why this clearly over-franked cover was marked for surcharge in the UK..

*From a set of 4 philatelic covers with the other Tristan da Cunha cancel of 1948 "Settlement of Edinburgh South Atlantic". These bear a clear Cape Town Paquebot transit mark. It is not clear why the 2½d cover was **not** surcharged!*

Varieties and Flaws on the Stamps

W. G. Stitt Dibden lists a large number of constant printing flaws. It has to be said that most of these are minor, and are not listed in current specialist catalogues.

2½d Value Flaws

1. **"Hole in ear"** flaw, cyl. 2 stop. 16/3: a coloured oval on lobe of King's ear.

2. **"Nick in ear"** flaw (*aside*), cyl. 2 stop. 19/1: a wedge-shaped coloured mark at lobe edge of King's ear

3. **"Extra Berry"** flaw (*below*), cyls. 2 and 3 no stop. 19/1: an uncoloured area at fourth leaf down, on right of right-hand laurel spray

4. **"Small Island"** cyl. 2 stop 17/5: a small coloured dot below the South-East coast of Africa and near Madagascar on the globe

5. **"Shade Change"** of background: a long wavy line through 'rings' and word 'Games'. Mostly on stamps cyl. 2 stop. 20/1 and 20/2 ➔

6. **"Small Island"** (Fig. 4) Cyl. 3 no stop. 12/2: a small coloured dot off the West coast of Africa, on the globe.

7. **Small coloured dot and slight bulge**: in left down-stroke of letter "A" of 'Games', cyl. 2 no stop. 1/4

8. **Etched amendments to 'box'** at peg hole in left margin, on cyls. 2 and 3 no stop

9. **Faulty "bottom bar"** below stamp cyl. 2 no stop. 20/4

10. **Two "coloured dots"** attached to and below right arm of centre bottom arrow in margin, on cyl. 2 no stop

11. **Large spot of colour** completely cutting lobe of King's ear, 4/1 cyl. 2 stop

3d Value Flaws & Varieties

1. **"Broken crown"** flaw (*aside*); cyl. 1 no stop. 20/2. A large uncoloured area appears at the left on the jewelled band of the crown. Contrary to common assumption, the flaw was not retouched: the flaw is not visible on lower numbered sheets, but quickly developed during the print run, and appears on at least 100,000 of the 125,000 sheets from this cylinder. The illustration shows the full state (left inset) and the developing state (right inset). There is also a large coloured dot in margin, below the stamp, throughout.
   The variety is found on stamps overprinted for **Morocco Agencies, Muscat** and **Tangier**.

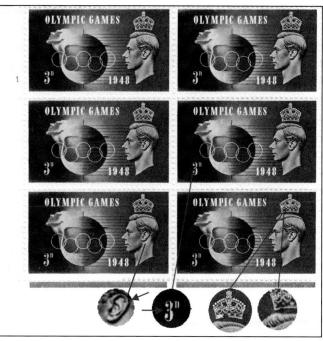

2. **"Hooked serif on 3"** (*aside*); cyl. 1 no stop. 19/2 Serif at centre of "**3**" instead of a straight line.

3. Horizontal lines trailing away from globe: the second line from the top completely broken about 1½ mm after leaving the globe Cyl. 1 no stop 4/5.

4. **"Double Line"** cyl. 1 stop. 20/6. A coloured oblique line below, and partly joining the normal one between right-hand ring and the King's lips.

5. **"Break"** in top line down just to right of World, Cyl. 1 stop 18/3

6. **"Break"** in second line down to right of world Cyl. 1 no stop 17/5

7. **Dark coloured dot** (*above*) on upper part of King's ear. Cyl. 1 no stop 20/1.

8. **"Cut"** in King's forehead A coloured mark, cyl. 1 no stop 20/3.

9. **"Retouched"** photogravure arrow in left margin, etched over and outlined on cyl. 1 no stop.

10. Retouched **"box"** at peg hole in left margin, etched over on cyl. 1 no stop.

Cadbury Brothers, Bourneville
CB *perfin*
B

All values were overprinted 'SPECIMEN' *for distribution to UPU member postal administrations.*

All values were overprinted 'SCHOOL SPECIMEN' *for training purposes* (N.B. the example illustrated is not authenticated)

6d Value Flaws & Varieties

1. Letters **"H L P"** on right-hand end of jubilee lines below stamps cyl. 9 stop. 20/4, 20/5, 20/6. This appears on a small number of sheets in the early period of printing. It was retouched out but traces remain. The letters are believed to stand for "Harrison London Printers" but it is also suggested they stand for engraver "H L Palmer". 3 (or 4) coloured dots in a straight line, appear in bottom margin below stamp 20/6 throughout. The fourth dot sometimes appears in the top margin above stamp 1/6.
    This variety occurs on some sheets used to print the **TANGIER** overprint, on others the lines have been retouched. For **Kuwait**, only the retouch has been seen.

2. Uncoloured Bulge on left side of top loop to figure 8 of "1948" Cyl. 9 no stop. 14/3.

3. The Jubilee lines below the bottom row on sheets numbered around 010020 show irregularities, Cyl.9 no stop. The lines below the second and third stamps taper off towards each other; below the last stamp the line is shortened, terminating below numeral "4" of "1948".

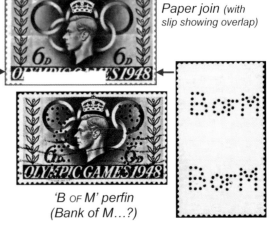

Paper join (with slip showing overlap)

'B OF M' perfin
(Bank of M…?)

1/- Value Flaws & Varieties

1. **"Extended Cornwall"** Cyl. 3 stop. 7/3. A large uncoloured area, attached to the Cornish coast of England, projects towards the Atlantic and South -East Ireland on the Globe.

2. **Uncoloured dot** below figure 1 and tail to figure 9 of "1948": Cyl. 3 stop 8/4.

Paper fold causing missing perforations—similar corner folds occur on all values

Double Surcharges

A part-sheet with a second surcharge top left, running into the margin was purchased at Kabrit on Bahrain Island. Another, with surcharge more to the right was purchased at Al Muharraq. 15 used examples are known, 13 on one cover!

3. **Dot by Finland** on the edge of the globe: Cyl. 3 no stop 18/3

4. **"Break in wing"**: Cyl. 3 stop. 1/3. A break and small coloured markings in the fourth horizontal line on left wing of the running figure.

5. A **Swollen Head** variety occurs on Cyl. 3 no stop 19/2.

6. **Spike below wing** on left side of figure Cyl. 3 no stop 7/3.

7. A fine **vertical line of colour** through King's head from the base of the neck, Cyl. 3 no stop 10/2 and 11/2.

One sheet of Morocco Agencies 1pta 20cts is reported (No. 012386 cyl. 3)

As few as 5 mint copies of the Muscat 1 rupee doubled surcharge may exist

Air letter Varieties

There is one variety arising from normal printing: an intense aniline ink was used for a small part of the run. This is impossible to detect with certainty with the naked eye, but is apparent under ultra-violet light.

The main varieties arise from the fact that the stamp impression was by Harrison, in photogravure, while the airletter itself was printed by letterpress by McCorquodale. Registration difficulties were feared, and indeed occurred.

The stamp impression is commonly found off-centre, sometimes mis-placed upwards, more often downwards, and extending outside the designated area. In a few instances the stamp is displaced about 22mm downwards and 7mm to the left, and falling across the dotted address lines.

A small number are known with the stamp entirely missing. In one instance the purchaser persuaded the counter clerk to apply his date-stamp in the space and the letter is postmarked "Maida Vale B.O.W. 9 / 6 OC 48".

One dramatic example is also reported where the stamp is in the correct position, but the light-blue shading and dark-blue text is printed upside-down, the relationship between the stamp impression and the gummed flaps confirming that it was correctly printed, but the blue was inverted.

Two private **overprints** are also known:

- a "FIRST DAY AIR LETTER" overprint depicting a runner, by J.D. Davidson, Stamp Dealer, 61 Rosemount Viaduct, Aberdeen. These are postmarked Aberdeen, and addressed to a Mrs Craig in South Africa.

- "Aero Field Christmas Greetings 1948" sent by the publishers of "The Aero Field" (Messrs David Field Ltd)

Presentation Cards, Packs and Folders

Although official presentation packs were not to be issued for another 16 years, there is an interesting variety of packs and cards carrying the 1948 Olympic stamps. The packs and cards illustrated are unique to the Olympic issue.

Special Issue of Postage Stamps

A pack produced in a numbered edition of 110 and containing the British stamps and the overprints for the 5 territories, in glassine pockets. It is believed to have been produced by Harrison's for dignitaries.

OLYMPIC GAMES

With Best Wishes for Christmas and the New Year

Aeronautical & General Instruments Limited
CROYDON · ENGLAND

A Christmas card produced by AGI. The stamps are affixed by hinges.

Harrison & Sons Ltd produced presentation cards for use by their salesmen to show their royal patronage, and to indicate the quality of their work to prospective customers. These were printed as required, and Olympic stamps were used for many years, at least until the mid-1950s. It is reported that there are around a dozen different styles of card bearing the Olympic stamps. Illustrated are two cards printed specifically to carry the set of Olympic stamps, and a generic card that happens to have two Olympic stamps.

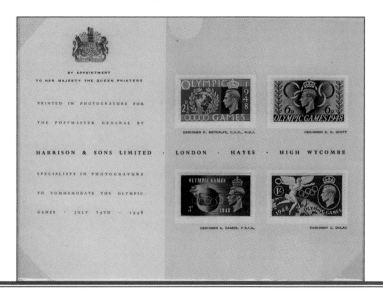

Pack produced by the GPO for ITTC delegates in 1949. The stamps are in glassine pockets. The folder was presented in a plain envelope with the name and address of the delegate written by hand.

First Day and Commemorative Covers

There was no official first day cover on sale in the Olympic Post Office, nor an official first day postmark (just the machine cancel in use throughout the Games). This particularly surprised overseas visitors who expected that a full philatelic service would be available for such an event of world-wide importance. Many will have known of the outstanding philatelic service provided at the previous Olympic Games, those of Berlin in 1936. The German Post Office was perhaps too exuberant, but the GPO's ultra-conservative policy went to the other extreme. One dealer at least solved the problem by waiting outside the Olympic P.O. and selling pictorial covers a-plenty to the disappointed customers as they came out.

This chapter illustrates the principal covers available, with details of their source or origin, where known. Some hand-drawn designs may be unique, or have been produced in very limited numbers. It is quite likely that there will be covers in this category not listed here. Covers were used not just on the first day, but throughout the Games, until the Closing Ceremony on 14 August.

FDC 1: This is the most commonly seen design, but this particular cover is an exceptionally early mailing, with the Olympic postmark of 8:45 a.m. on 29 July. Now the Olympic P.O. was not open until 9 a.m. London Chief Office in King Edward Street will have been selling the Olympic stamps from midnight, otherwise the post offices in the Olympic Villages at Richmond, Uxbridge and Drayton Park were open from 8 a.m., so it is possible the sender came from there to Wembley. The third possibility is that the cover and remittance were mailed in in advance, and the stamps affixed by Wembley P.O. staff.

FDC 1a: Cover with dry-print red (feint impressions of the red text and rings can be seen on the original)

FDC 2: Published by Jim Davis Ltd., stamp dealers; no doubt the one on sale outside the Olympic P.O.

FDC 3: *British Philatelic Association and Philatelic Traders' Society.*
FDC 3a: *the same design in shades of grey as a label on a cover mailed in Chesterfield*

FDC 4: *Tower Bridge (boxed) design by John Verhoeven (USA)*
FDC 4a: *the same design unboxed (smaller envelope)*

Hand coloured example addressed to a relative of the artist, and possibly mailed by the artist himself.

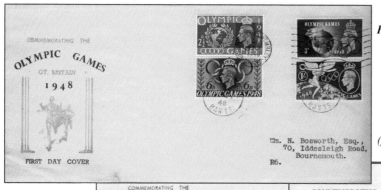

FDC 5a: *Runners between pillars; gold and dark blue on DL-sized envelope.*
FDC 5b: *dark beige and green*
FDC 5b2: *C6-size envelope*
FDC 5c: *mauve and dark blue*

FDC 6: *Runners at the tape (green) [same drawing as FDC 5]*

Note non-Olympic Wembley wavy line postmark

FDC 7: *Artcraft cover, from the USA, and pre-paid postcard advertising the envelopes.*

FDC 8: *Fosters (DL) Flame in bowl on plinth with rings*

FDC 9: *Fosters (small, 153 x 90mm)*

FDC 10: *David J. Hume Ltd (Stamp Fair)*

(a) *195 x 127mm (filler shown is for American market)*

(b) *155 x 100mm (example shown is hand-coloured, possibly by the addressee)*

FDC 11: *Torch within a wreath, in blue-grey*

FDC 12: *Malling (Maidstone)*

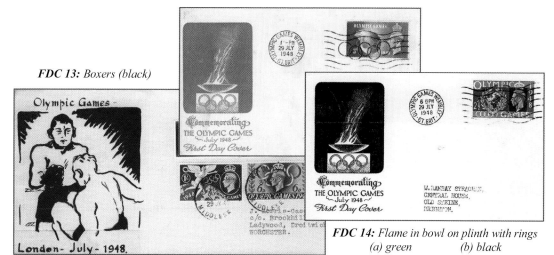

FDC 13: *Boxers (black)*

FDC 14: *Flame in bowl on plinth with rings*
(a) green   (b) black

FDC 15: *The London Assurance, text and coat of arms in green, plus folded paper insert. Note that two sets of the stamps were enclosed.*

FDC 16: *Mercury in grey-blue.*
Published by Stamp Collecting Ltd.

FDC 17: *Runner under crossed Union flags*

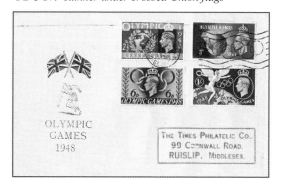

FDC 18: *Discus thrower and pillar with Olympic Rings "First Day Cover" framed and in fancy font above the image.*
    a)   in blue-grey
    b)   In dull-orange
    c)   In purple-brown
FDC 19: *Same image, but in brown, and slightly larger and "FIRST DAY COVER" in plain font bottom centre.*

FDC 20: *Runner with shadow; red text*   **FDC 21:** *Hand-drawn cauldron & rings, typed text*

FDC 22: *Wembley Stadium Ltd*

FDC 23: *Coloured rings; typed bottom left*
"XIVTH OLYMPIAD / WEMBLEY"

FDC 24: *Hurdler and Rings in black*

FDC 25: *North Herts Stamp Club*
(green & black)

FDC 26: *Exmouth Stamp Club*
(printed 'July 1st' corrected by typewriter)

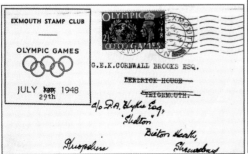

FDC 27: *Medway Towns Philatelic Society*

FDC 28: *High-jumper and diver (black, red text)*

FDC 29: *Bulldog and flags*

FDC 30: *Rings and Globe (hand-coloured, oversize)*

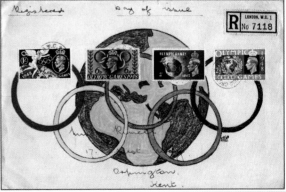

FDC 31: *Badge with Big Ben and Rings (hand-coloured)*

FDC 32: *Boxed hurdler with cyclist, boxer and footballer. Addressed to Renown Stamp Co Ltd*

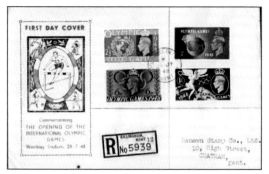

FDC 33: *Rings, motto, date and text all in purple*

FDC 34: *Wm S. Linto cachet—flag and text in brown (publisher's details on reverse)*

FDC 35: *Hurdler in black*

FDC 36: *Flag and discus thrower, blue text (note Wembly [sic] red frame*

FDC 36a: *Postmarked Olympia Fields Illinois*

FDC 37: *British Broadcasting Corporation*

Postal Arrangements—
Venues and Villages

Postal, telegraph and telephone communication facilities for the Games were the responsibility of the General Post Office (GPO), and are set out in detail in the Official Report of the Games. Discussions with the Organising Committee began in January 1947, a working committee was set up, there was wide-ranging consultation, particularly with British and international press organisations, and as a result, the GPO was able to form a clear picture of the magnitude of the traffic which might be generated, and how it might be divided between the different media—postal, telegraph, teleprinter and telephone. This book concentrates on the postal.

Counter at the special Olympic Post Office, Wembley

Post Office Magazine, October, 1948

Temporary Post Offices

Special Olympic post offices were opened as follows:

Wembley	July 27 & 28	noon—6 p.m.
	July 29—Aug 14	9 a.m.—10 p.m.
Torquay	July 10—Aug 12	8 a.m.—6 p.m.
Bisley	July 26—Aug 14	10 a.m.—9 p.m.
Richmond Park	July 5—Aug 21	8 a.m.—2 p.m.
Housing Centre		6 p.m.—8 p.m.
Uxbridge	July 8—Aug 21	8 a.m.—2 p.m.
Housing Centre		6 p.m.—8 p.m.
West Drayton	July 8—Aug 21	8 a.m.—noon
Housing Centre		1 p.m.—2 p.m.
		6 p.m.—8 p.m.
Henley	5—7 August	Mobile PO 2
Aldershot	9—13 August	Mobile PO 2

Not included in this list is the post office serving the Earls Court Exhibition Halls which it is understood was open while the Weightlifting events were held in the Empress Hall on 31st July and 2nd and 3rd August, and possibly gymnastics (moved there from the Stadium).

Wembley

The main Olympic Post Office was located in the Civic Hall, within the Stadium grounds on one of the main approaches to the Stadium. The main public office was about 670 square feet (62m^2), with a 29-foot counter accommodating six counter positions. There was also a public telephone hall and a large telegraph instrument room. This initially had three teleprinters for the transmission of telegrams, but after two or three days this was reduced to two, anticipated press usage not materialising, the press phoning reports, or using direct lines of private telegraph companies installed at Wembley.

A small public office was provided in the Stadium itself, primarily as a telegraph office for the press, but also selling stamps. This was situated in the Long Bar, behind two Tote windows, and open from an hour before events until one hour after they finished, but did very little business. Any one of the counter handstamps from the main Olympic post office was borrowed as occasion demanded.

Wembley Stadium and the Civic Hall
(Private photograph in private collection)

Although the Olympic post office and its staff came under the administration of Wembley Head Office, the actual personnel came from all regions of the UK, a Post Office Circular having sought volunteers (linguistic qualifications were desirable). The full complement of the postal side at the Olympic branch office was:

1 Assistant Superintendent

2. Overseers

14. Postal & Telegraph Officers for the counter work.

2 Interpreters

2 Postmen, Higher Grade

2 Postmen (for collections from the special boxes)

1 Postman (for clearing telephone coin boxes)

4. Young Postmen (for telegraph delivery within the grounds and taking telegrams from the Telegraph Annexe in the Stadium to the post office in the grounds—a pipe was rigged up, telegrams being lowered in a carrier from the first floor to the ground floor, to save time mounting and descending the stairs.)

2 Kiosk Cleaners

2 Office Cleaners

A number of Telegraphists (later reduced).

Business was slack in the two days before the Games opened, but on 29 July the post office was extremely busy all day long. Thereafter the office was busiest in the three hours before the afternoon session at the Stadium, and for an hour or so after the last event. Little business was done after 9 p.m. on most days.

There was no cancelling machine, and no sorting facilities in the Olympic office, so a relay of two vans ran to and from the sorting office at Wembley Head Office. On the first day of issue of the stamps and use of the special machine cancel, 29 July, the opening day of the Games, some of the covers were then taken on to Harrow sorting office where one of the Olympic dies and daters was fitted in a cancelling

The Olympic Post Office, with stamp vending machine, and pillar box with for mail to receive the Olympic slogan

machine. Bulk mailings received from commercial firms were also sent to Harrow.

The GPO had no philatelic section, and was only vaguely aware of the needs of philatelists. Foreign collectors in particular were amazed and disappointed that there were no official first day covers available (one enterprising dealer set himself up outside and sold pictorial covers at a steady pace). Collectors were even more disappointed that there was no special handstamp available, and no hand-back service, the only Olympic postmark being a machine cancel applied to mail posted in one of six specially designated boxes. These bore notices in English, French, and Spanish to indicate that items posted in the box would receive the Olympic postmark.

The Olympic Post Office postmaster and some of his staff, standing beside one of the designated post boxes; note the tri-lingual notice affixed to the top of the box

The six boxes were located as follows:

1. Outside the Olympic PO in the Civic Hall

2. On the green between the Civic Hall and the Empire Pool (Swimming and boxing venue)

3. Wembley Park Station end of Olympic way

4. Wembley Arena end of Olympic Way

5. Adjoining the kennels opposite Wembley railway station

6. Opposite the Royal Tunnel entrance to the Stadium

Collectors were very disappointed to discover that the Olympic postmark was not available (on a hand-back basis) in the Olympic P.O, and even more dismayed that registered letters would not receive an Olympic postmark. Instead they would be cancelled at the counter with a standard "WEMBLEY MIDDLESEX" circular date stamp. These were numbered 11—16. Some collectors decided to post prepared registered envelopes marked with blue lines in one of the special postboxes in order to get them franked with the Olympic machine postmark. This sometimes had the unfortunate effect for the recipient that somewhere in the mail system the envelope would be recognised as a registered letter that had got in the ordinary mail system and was not being given secure treatment. It would be pulled out and marked "POC 3^D to pay" for "posted out of course". A local registration label would be applied and (often) a postage due stamp. The recipient would have to pay the surcharge even if the letter bore a full set of Olympic stamps and so was considerably overpaid, even for registered mail. (One cover is known where an Australian registration label was applied in Melbourne, but it was not surcharged.) Express letters handed over also just received a counter c.d.s. cancel.

The photograph of the counter at the Olympic PO taken from the Post Office Magazine, October 1948 shows a sign above the counter. It starts "We are sorry that the SPECIAL OLYMPIC POSTMARKS cannot be …". The rest of the text is sadly illegible. It seems unlikely that the sign was in place when the office opened, but it was no doubt hurriedly made following the problems on the first day.

There was also an experimental Parcel Post Label printing machine at the Olympic P.O. counter. The adhesive labels showed the price and date, and did not need to be cancelled. Only 23 parcels were accepted, the machine frequently broke down, so it is not known how many of the parcels actually received the label. (The machine was transferred to Wembley Head Office counter after the Games, and was in use intermittently until at least 1955). There was also a huge multi-value franking machine used for franking telegraph forms instead of using postage stamps.

The GPO had estimated that a quarter of a million first day covers would be posted and made arrangements accordingly. This was a gross over-estimate, only 66,475 being recorded. Over the whole period of the Games total mail recorded was just 182,529 items.

Wembley Olympic Postings

29 July	Wembley	45,479
	To Harrow	20,996
30 July		4,407
31 July		6,267
1 August		364
2 August		6,464
3 August		11,530
4 August		11,194
5 August		10,081
6 August		10,076
7 August		11,216
8 August		545
9 August		7,561
10 August		7,364
11 August		5,996
12 August		4,579
13 August		6,681
14 August		11,729

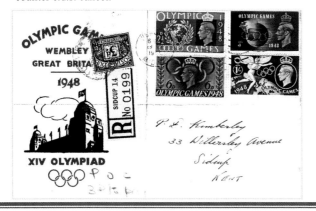

OLYMPIC GAMES   POSTAL ARRANGEMENTS

1. Olympic B.O.) - Open 27th and 28th July, Noon to 6.0 p.m.
   Civic Hall   )
   Wembley   ) - Open 29th July to 14th August, 9.0 a.m. to 10.0 p.m.
                     (Sundays excepted).

2. Olympic B.O. box to be brought into use after the final collection 28th July.
   Other special boxes to be opened after final collection 28th, when special
   notices will be fixed to all special boxes by the Engineers.

3. The collection from the special boxes will be at normal times plus a 7.30 p.m.
   collection from boxes other than that at the B.O. where the final advertised
   collection will be 8.0 p.m.

4. From 29th July to 14th August, a collection from the B.O. will be required at
   10 p.m. except on Sundays.

5. On 29th July a P.H.G. (one early) 9.0 a.m. to 5.0 p.m. (O.T. if necessary)
   to be employed at the B.O. for bagging registered items and dealing with bagging
   bulk postings.

6. Three additional official mail vans will be available during the period 29th
   July to 14th August for use on collections, conveyance and coin collecting duties,
   one van will normally be parked at the Civic Hall, Wembley, for emergencies, i.e.
   collections, conveyance or coin collecting, etc., as required.

7. Postman Driver with van at the B.O. from 6.0 a.m. on 29th to receive bulk
   postings. Another Postman Driver with van to clear special boxes from 6.0 a.m.
   Proceeds of collections to be conveyed at frequent intervals to Wembley Office.

8. A/Inspr. on duty supervising stamping arrangements at Wembley all day from
   6.30 a.m. to 10.0 p.m. on 29th July only. A/Inspr. as above for duty 8.30 a.m.
   to 4.30 p.m. and O.T. for remaining period, (to be withdrawn if not found to be
   warranted).

9. A/Inspr. supervising stamping to ensure that in the event of an accumulation
   of work items proper to a timed collection are not mixed with items from a subsequent collection. To ensure that date-stamp time changes are made after all
   items proper to bear a specific time impression have been stamped. To arrange
   for frequent despatches of available work to Harrow, and to notify the Inspector,
   sorting duties, Harrow, when all items proper to a particular collection have
   been despatched. To take hourly readings of stamping machine, and personally to
   ensure that changes in time stamps are recorded on a special date-stamp impression sheet and the machine is in order before any letters are passed through the
   machine.

10. After letters have been machine stamped, all letters are to be examined before
    sortation or despatch to ensure that all items bear a machine stamping impression,
    items which have failed stamping should be returned to the machine, and items
    which have some stamps so placed that they are not cancelled by the machine are
    to be thrown out for hand-stamping. The ink on the pads used for machine and
    hand stamping should not be wet, and every effort must be made to ensure that a
    surplus of ink is not impressed.

11. An additional stamping machine and facing table will be installed in Wembley
    Sorting Office for use during the period 29th July to 14th August.

12. Six additional Facers have been recruited, normal hours of attendance 12.30
    p.m. to 8.30 p.m., but on 29th July, 6.30 a.m. to 2.30 p.m. On 29th July O.T.
    to be arranged for facing after 2.30 p.m.

13. Reserve Olympic stamp cancelling machine dies will be held at Harrow H.O. and
    London E.C.D.O. for use if the volume of letters to be stamped exceeds the
    capacity of the Wembley arrangements. No correspondence is to be diverted to
    London E.C.D.O. without the prior authority of the Superintendent, Harrow.
    Letters diverted to Harrow or E.C. must be clearly labelled "Olympic postings
    for Special Die to be stamped ....(a.m./p.m.) ....(date)".

    Correspondence forwarded to E.C.D.O. for stamping must be forwarded by official
    mail van, the driver to be provided with a Way Bill, and the platform Overseer
    (Telephone   ) must be advised by telephone prior to the driver's
    departure.

14. Supplementary collections will be made from boxes in the neighbourhood of the
    Stadium and its approaches, i.e. London Bridge, Wembley Park Station, Empire
    Way, Dagmar Avenue, Wembley Hill T.S.O., The Mall, 180, High Road T.S.O., High
    Road.

15. Letter and Parcel Delivery Arrangements.

    All letters and parcels for competitors coming to hand at Wembley not bearing
    a normal address in the town or addressed Wembley Stadium, Pool or Olympics, to
    be forwarded to London, E.C. for redirection, bundles of letters to be forwarded
    in unsealed enclosure bags labelled "Correspondence for redirection - Olympic
    competitors". All items forwarded to be examined first by A/Inspr. to ensure

Senior off. on Duty E.C.S.O. Central 2040 EX4131/0 EX4131/

that/

To be Labeled OLYMPIC POSTINGS

.... COLLECTION.

that correspondence which is proper for delivery in Wembley is not sent to E.C.

Letters for the "Press Centre", Civic Hall, to be delivered to the Steward at the Press Centre.

16. Two P.H.G.s (one early, one late) to be at the B.O. from 29th July to 14th August, for supervision of Boy Messengers.

17. Telegrams delivered from the Olympic B.O. will be to the Press Centre and Olympic Games Committee only, both situated in the Civic Hall. Two early Messengers and two late.

18. Four Boy Messengers as follows - 2 (one early, one late) stationed outside P.O. in the Long Bar in the Wembley Stadium for transferring messages from P.O. to gravity tube to hut below, and 2 (one early, one late) to be stationed in hut on ground level outside Stadium to receive messages from gravity tube and convey them to the Instrument Room in the B.O. premises for transmission.

19. An electric coin counting machine will be installed at Wembley J.H.Q. for use during the period 29th July to 14th August.

20. Two full-time Cleaners will be employed at the Olympic B.O. and three additional kiosk cleaners will be operating in the Exhibition Grounds and Stadium to service the additional telephone kiosks.

21. Arrangements will be made for the Wembley J.H.Q. counter to be fully staffed during the period of the Games and for two Counter officers who will be employed at Wembley J.H.Q. to attend a special one day course on Monday, 26th July, on the acceptance of Press and Foreign Telegrams.

22. On 29th July, an A/Inspr. to be on duty from 9.0 a.m. to 5.0 p.m. at the Olympic B.O. to control queues at the public counter.

23. Two Counter positions, opposite the Long Bar in the Stadium will be staffed whilst events are in progress in the Stadium, for the acceptance of telegrams and the sale of stamps.

24. All officers employed at the B.O. and Stadium will be able to obtain meals at the Civic Hall, the premises will be pointed out by the Officer i/C. of the B.O., from whom vouchers for meals may be obtained on payment of the requisite amount. Personnel (except Boy Messengers) under the control of the Officer i/C. Olympic B.O. will be entitled to the "Special Event" subsistence rate of 7d. per hour, for Boy Messengers the rate is 3d. per hour.

25. All officers whose duties necessitate their attendance inside the Stadium will be issued with Special Passes of Admission.

26. There is no accommodation for the storage of private cycles at the Olympic B.O.

Typed and duplicated details of the postal arrangements kept by the Wembley Postmaster. On the back are proof impressions of the Olympic machine cancels and four skeleton cancellers. There are also manuscript notes, and a record of items mailed (in blue ink). This is a unique record.

(Private collection)

Incoming Mail and Other Venues

The Organising Committee did not allocate teams to the various 'Housing Centres' until shortly before the Games when numbers were known, so each country's team was given a London EC box number, with incoming mail to be addressed as follows:

> Name of Competitor (or Team Official)
> Olympic Team of …………….
> Box ….
> London, E.C.1, England

The Organising Committee informed the Post Office of the actual locations, so enabling the forwarding of mail. Because teams and team members arrived at different times (some as early as May), Richmond Park centre was opened on 10 June. Some athletes initially installed there had to be moved later to balance the accommodation and enable teams to be kept together. About 3,000 letters a day were received and forwarded, and about 150 parcels all told. Mail and telegrams were delivered to the respective 'Centre Commandant' for final distribution.

The main centres were the RAF camps of **Uxbridge** and **West Drayton** and the military camp in **Richmond Park**, housing 1,600, 700 and 1,600 men respectively. Each had a post office (which was not open to the general public). No more than three counter positions were required at any of them.

Other accommodation was in schools in Middlesex for the men, 18 schools in all, and three large private colleges for the women. None of these had postal facilities. Accommodation for **Aldershot** was in The Royal Military Academy at **Sandhurst**. For outgoing mail, a mobile post office was stationed in Aldershot for the equestrian events from 9—13 August (but not for the earlier modern pentathlon).

The yachtsmen in **Torquay** were accommodated in hotels. There was a temporary post office in Torquay, on the Marine Spa, and accessible to the public. It had an 18-foot counter, and a posting box was erected nearby. However there was no special postmark, and mail posted in the box received an ordinary Torquay wavy line cancel.

At **Bisley** the National Rifle Association camp provided suitable accommodation. The Olympic post office was the camp post office, opened regularly for competitions and events in the camp. It was open from 26 July to 14 August, but competition days were just 2—6 August.

Accommodation for the rowers and canoeists competing at **Henley** proved difficult. The principal accommodation was in 3 schools in **High Wycombe**, 10 miles away, with overspill in two other schools and a Government Camp. The very few women canoeists were accommodated in a hotel in Henley. No postal facilities were provided for competitors specifically. A mobile post office was stationed at Henley, reportedly just for the event days of 5-7 August, although the rowing finals were held on Monday 9 August and canoeing 11—12 August. The mobile post office moved on to **Aldershot** for these dates.

Business done at the Olympic Games Post Office at Wembley, and at the Post Offices in the Housing Centres (Villages) (Official Report)

Olympic Post Office	Value of stamps sold	No. of parcels accepted	No. of packets regis-tered	No. of transactions			No. of telegrams	
				Money Orders	Postal Orders	Saving Bank	For-warded	Re-ceived
	£							
Wembley	3,695	23	1,401	75	672	496	1,382	440
Richmond Park	1,679	570	962	31	283	—	716	2,550
Uxbridge	1,558	223	436	64	211	—	723	2,962
West Drayton	533	150	213	25	169	—	381	1,126
Totals …………….	7,465	966	3,012	195	1,335	496	3,202	7,078

Olympic Mail

Aerogramme sent from Bisley Camp on the first day of issue, 29 July, by A.E. Cook, future Gold Medallist in the 50m Small Bore Rifle event, giving his address as "U.S. Olympic Rifle Team, Box 1102, London EC1".

Cover from the Argentine Athletics Delegation mailed from Richmond Park Village on 11 July (Kingston-on-Thames wavy line postmark for mail placed in pillar boxes).

Olympic Postmarks and Registration Labels

Venues and Villages

Wembley Slogan

Three dies were cut with '**OLYMPIC GAMES WEMBLEY · GT.BRIT** ·' daters and Olympic rings between wavy lines. The Postmaster's notes, paragraph 13, indicate that one dater was at Wembley, and that "reserve Olympic stamp cancelling machine dies will be held at Harrow HO and London ECDO for use if the volume of letters to be stamped exceeds the capacity of the Wembley arrangements." Proofs were run off on the back of the notes. The first die (Die 1) was found to be OK, the

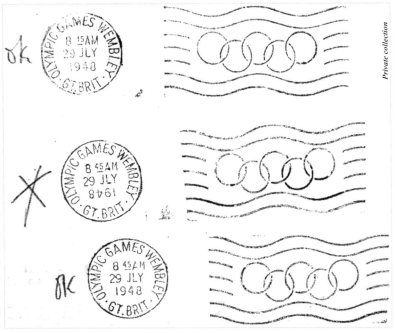

Private collection

second die initially had the year slug inverted, this was corrected, and this die was then found to be acceptable. This die, Die 2, was the one sent over to Harrow. The third die was never used.

Die 1 (above) and Die 2 at 1 –PM on 29 July, with enlarged copy to highlight differences.
Die 2 was first used at 1 –PM and quickly became mis-placed downwards in the machine.

The differences are very slight. Die 1 has a wider 'M' in OLYMPIC, with the uprights horizontal, a slanting 'M' in GAMES, and the lettering in WEMBLEY is slightly wider apart. In Die 2 the '*M*' in OLYMPIC slants downwards. In the Postmaster's proofs Die 1 has 'AM', Die 2 'AM' but this is not a constant: on 29 July at I−PM both are short, at $3^{\underline{45}}$ Die 1 has the short M, at $6^{\underline{15}}$ both are again short.

However at I−PM on 29 July Die 2 slipped down, and it is reported that this die did not fit well in the machine. Whether it was this factor or the reduced volume of mail, on subsequent days the postmaster's notes do not mention any mail going to Harrow. That said, Die 2 was in use at 1 −PM on 4 August. All other examples examined dated 30 July and after have been Die 1.

Another way of identifying Die 2 on 29 July is by any skeleton used to cancel stamps missed by the slogan. Harrow seem to have used Wembley skeletons with the date across the centre, as explained below.

Die 2, 4 August

There were no Olympic events on the Sundays 1 & 8 August. The Postmaster's notes record 364 and 545 items mailed. These were presumably cancelled on the day and forwarded through the mail, (Sunday collections were standard in 1948), but no examples have come to light to confirm this.

The Postmaster's manuscript notes show (weekday) times of cancellation as 8:45 (set from 8 am), 1 pm, 3:45, 6:15, and 8 pm. These times seem to have applied throughout the Olympic period. However, an additional time is found on 2 August, namely 5 pm.

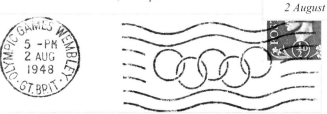

Die 1, 5 −PM, 2 August

Wembley Skeletons

The Postmaster's manuscript note refers to three steel and one rubber "stamp", and again impressions were made on the back of the notes. *P4* is distinctly different and is not a skeleton but a rubber packet cancel; only one actual example has come to light.

When it comes to actual examples, many can be found that do not correspond to the postmaster's impressions. It is clear that the lettering was not always tight, and different slots were used for date and time. There were also two Wembley skeletons in use at Harrow. It is not clear if either or both of these were sent over from Wembley.

Complete strikes are hard to find, which does not make the task of identifying the skeleton any easier. It is reported that for a brief period the letter 'M' of Middlesex was inverted, to produce 'Widdlesex'. However poor strikes can mean that the first stroke of 'M' does not register giving the appearance of a 'W', so exercise caution before spending a lot of money on an alleged 'Widdlesex'!

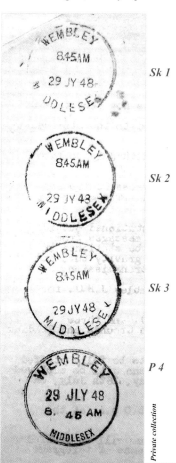

Sk 1

Sk 2

Sk 3

P 4

Private collection

Skeleton *Sk 1*

- WEMBLEY offset left (Y high)
- Time & date evenly spaced
- (A)M below EY above 4
- E high after S

Skeleton *Sk 2*

- WEMBLEY offset right (Y low); E touches M
- Time & date widely apart
- AM below LE above 48
- 48 below X close to S
- E lower than L

Skeleton *Sk 3*

- WEMBLEY offset left (Y high)
- Wide **M** of WE**M**BLEY
- Time & date widely apart
- Date higher than *Sk 2*;
- High E before S

Packet cancel *P 4*

- WEMBLEY large and spread out, MIDDLESEX small and compact
- Date has large digits and is above time; all appear to be on revolving loops)

Used in Harrow (no Postmaster's proof):

Skeleton *Sk H1*

- Wide **M** of WE**M**BLEY and **M**ID
- Date across the centre
- E high after L before S
- MIDDLESEX offset right (X high)

Skeleton *Sk H2*

- Wide **M** of WE**M**BLEY not MID
- Gap between time and date, which is just below centre
- MIDDLESEX more even

Skeletons in practice

Sk 1

- The earliest time seen is 1 pm on 29 July
- Note the dot after 1.

Sk 2

- The earliest time seen is 3:45 pm on 30 July

Sk 3

- The earliest time seen is also 1 pm on 29 July
- Note that WEMBLEY is more central than in the proof. This change seems consistent.
- *Sk3* was used 5pm on 2 August

P4

- This is the only example seen. The size of MIDDLESEX however suggests it may be a different packet cancel from the one tested by the postmaster.

Sk H1

- First use seen for H1 & H2 was 3:45 PM on 29 July

Sk H2

- On 12 August this appears on a cover from Wembley itself, with Die 1

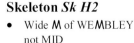

Double Ring Circular Date Stamps

Use of the skeletons is rare after 29-30 July. If the machine cancel has missed stamps it is far more common to see a WEMBLEY MIDDX double ring c.d.s. applied.

*The addressee of this cover with Die 1 slogan and double ring cds, **Béla Szepes**, won a Silver Medal in the javelin in Amsterdam in 1928, and was no doubt on the support team in 1948.*

A highly unusual combination: a set with first day machine cancel from Harrow (Die 2) at 6^{15} PM on a cover which apparently found its way back to Wembley, where it received a WEMBLEY MIDDLESEX cds timed at 7. PM.

Experimental Parcel Post Label

It is reported that 23 parcels were posted, but the experimental machine at the Olympic P.O. counter often broke down, so even fewer labels may have actually been used.

From Postmarks of England & Wales by James MacKay

Wembley Olympic P.O. Counter Hand-stamps & Registration Label

Mail handed over the counter of the Olympic Post Office received a 'WEMBLEY MIDDLESEX' cds numbered from 11-16, and a 'WEMBLEY 40' registration label was applied. Registered mail is scarce, but, ironically, registered first day covers posted at other Wembley post offices are even more scarce, and quite sought after.

Cover mailed in special posting box, with Olympic wavy line machine mark, (Die 2, Harrow) crossed for registration, Wembley 50 registration label applied in the sorting office and cover marked 'P. O. C. 3ᵈ TO PAY'; Irish postage due stamps applied.

Olympic Housing Centres

1.   Richmond Park

The Olympic Post office was open from 5 July to 21 August. The counter clerks used 'KINGSTON-ON-THAMES / SURREY' circular date stamps with numerals 9 or 10 above the date, and 'KINGSTON-ON-THAMES 33' registration labels.

Registered cover sent from Richmond Park Olympic Village by an Italian weightlifter, Guiseppe Colantuono , 'KINGSTON-ON-THAMES 9' cds & 'KINGSTON-ON-THAMES 33' R-label

A telegram sent to the Swedish Soccer Team received in the Richmond Park Olympic Village, with KINGSTON-ON-THAMES 10 cds arrival marker

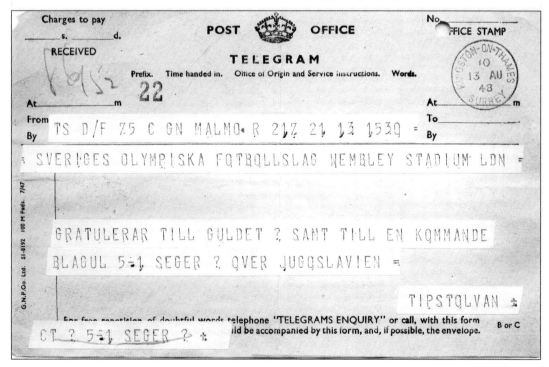

Postcard of the West Drayton RAF camp, before its conversion to Olympic accommodation.
Aerial photo of the Uxbridge Camp. The post office was in building '1', as was the main recreation
and writing room. The US team was largely housed here.

2. Uxbridge

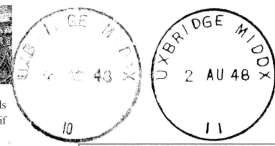

There were two skeletons for use at the counter, numbered 10 & 11, and 'UXBRIDGE 28' R-labels were used. Mail put in the post box received a normal wavy-line machine cancel. (The cds illustrated is from competitor's mail; it is not known if it is from the Village temporary P.O.)

3. West Drayton

West Drayton had three 'WEST DRAYTON MIDDX' skeletons (nos. 6, 7, & 8) and 'WEST DRAYTON 5' R-labels.

Note that '6' has the date in two lines.

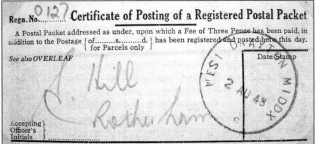

4. High Wycombe

There were no dedicated postal facilities for the three schools in High Wycombe used to house competitors for the rowing and canoeing events. Mail therefore received normal postal markings. However, competitors were presented with a postcard of the Henley Regatta Course [*see postcard chapter*] to which a special rubber cachet was applied. (They were also presented with an attractive 32-page A4 size brochure with black and white photos of High Wycombe and Henley)

Olympic Venue Post Offices

1.   Torquay

At Torquay, the yachting venue, there was a temporary Olympic post office at the Marine Spa, open from 10 July to 12 August. Yachting events took place from 3—6 August, and 10—12 August.

Ordinary mail posted there received the normal wavy line postmark, but registered mail posted at the counter received a 'TORQUAY' cds with a star '*' above the date, and a 'TORQUAY A' R-label with numbers in the 5000s.

This attractive first day cover was not mailed from the temporary post office at the Marine Spa, but from the main Torquay post office; the date-stamp has no '' and the TORQUAY A registration label has too high a number.*

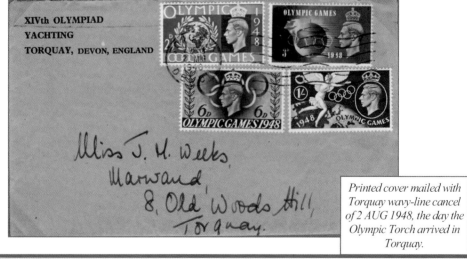

Printed cover mailed with Torquay wavy-line cancel of 2 AUG 1948, the day the Olympic Torch arrived in Torquay.

2. Mobile Post Office 2—

a. Henley

A mobile P.O. was stationed at Henley for the rowing events from 5—7 August only. It had moved on by Finals day, Monday 9 August, and did not return for the canoeing 11—12 August.

Two circular date stamps are known to have been used at the counter: 'MOBILE POST OFFICE 2' 'A' and 'C'. 'HENLEY-ON-THAMES P' registration labels were used.

b. Aldershot

MPO 2 moved on to Aldershot and was there for the equestrian events from 9—13 August. There was no mobile P.O. for the modern pentathlon events between 30 July and 4 August.

The same counter handstamps will have been used, with a large blank registration label with details inserted in manuscript.

(MPO 2 was located at Burnley for the Royal Lancashire Agricultural Show from 28 July— 2 August. MPO 1 was at Bridgend for the National Eisteddfod of Wales from 31 July—7 August. Covers from these dates will not therefore be Olympic.)

3. Bisley Camp

Bisley Camp post office was opened each summer during major shooting competitions, and was open for the Olympics between July 26 & 14 August.

Counter mail received a single-ring cds cancel, and registered mail a 'WOKING 7' R-label. Mail posted in the camp post box received a double-ring cds cancel.

Other Venues

There were no special postal facilities or Olympic post offices at venues other than Wembley, Aldershot, Bisley, and Henley, but first day covers and other postal items can be found, and make an interesting feature of any collection:

Note the Federation Internationale de Basketball Amateur cachet, and 'POOC' marking..

Air Letter mailed from North Finchley, & extract from message

FDC from regular Earls Court PO

Basketball—Harringay Arena, 6—14 August

- Nearest post office **Finsbury Park**

Boxing—Empire Pool, Wembley 9—13 August

Fencing-Palace of Engineering, Wembley 30 July—13 August

Football—Empire Stadium, Wembley 30 July—7 August, 10, 11 & 13 August

Hockey—Empire Stadium, Wembley 9 & 12 August

Swimming, Diving & Water Polo— Empire Pool, Wembley 29 July—7 August

- Served by **Wembley Olympic Post Office**

Swimming & Water Polo Preliminaries— Finchley Pool

- **North Finchley P.O.**

Cycling—Herne Hill 7, 9 & 11 August

- **Herne Hill P.O.**

Cycling—Windsor Great Park— Road Race 13 August

- **Windsor P.O.**

Wrestling—Empress Hall, Earls Court, 29 July—5 August

Weightlifting— Empress Hall, Earls Court 31 July, 2 & 3 August

Gymnastics—Empress Hall, Earls Court 9—11 August (*change—waterlogged Stadium*)

- **Earls Court Exhibition P.O.**

Postage Meters
(franking machine impressions)

Box Office Meter

Depicting the Olympic Rings in a running track, this was used from December 1947, and is regularly found on buff envelopes with printed logo.

Later, the Box Office used a 'regular' meter advertising greyhound racing at the stadium.

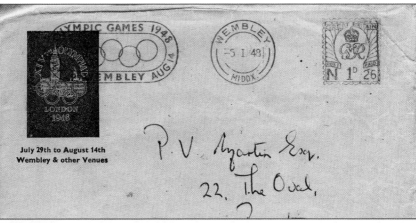

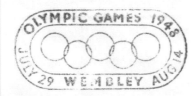 

The Rank Organisation

Rank made or distributed the Olympic film.

Longines

Official Watch for the 1948 U.S. Olympic Committee

The Torch Relay—from Olympia to London and Torquay—
& the Opening Ceremony

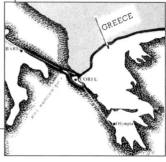

The Olympic Torch Relay was introduced in 1936 for the Berlin Games, and on 17 July1948 the Flame was lit for a second time for the relay to London.

Political unrest in Greece meant the Torch was unable to go from Olympia to Athens, so it was taken straight to the Greek coast at Katakolon, some 22 miles from Olympia, then on by the Greek destroyer Hastings to Corfu. From there it was carried by the frigate HMS Whitesand Bay to Bari in Italy, whence runners took it through Ancona, Bologna and Milan to the Simplon Pass and then into

Souvenir cards with regular Olympia cancels (top), and indecipherable cancel (below).

Handstamp from Olympia, including a Torch (rare), on souvenir card with arrival cancel from Pyrgos (on the Torch Relay route).

Private postcard of HMS Whitesand Bay (from the collection of Oscar Parkes, former Editor of Jane's Fighting Ships)

COMITATO OLIMPICO NAZIONALE ITALIANO

ROMA - STADIO NAZIONALE - ROMA

Mr.F.W.COLLINS
Commander, R.N. (Retd)
Organiser;, Torch Relay

Organising Committee for
the XlV^ Olympiad

37, Upper Brook Street

= LONDON W.1. =

(Inghilterra)

Switzerland. In Lausanne, Madame la Baronne de Coubertin was present at a ceremony held at *Mon Repos*, the IOC headquarters. There was a further ceremony in the cemetery where her late husband Baron Pierre de Coubertin is buried, then the Torch proceeded through Geneva to the French border at St. Julien. It proceeded through eastern France to Luxembourg, then Belgium, returning to France near Lille and on to Calais, where it was carried on board HMS Bicester at 6:15pm on 28 July.

Letter from the Italian Olympic Committee to the organiser of the Torch Relay, Commander Collins (there were no Italian postmarks for the Relay). Note the coincidental use of three Torch definitives.

Postcard published for the 2012 Torch Relay reproducing a 1948 photo showing the Torch leaving HMS Bicester on arrival at Dover (highlighted).

Contemporary postcard-sized photo of HMS Bicester by Wright & Logan, Southsea

It arrived in Dover at 8:25pm that evening, and after a short ceremony, proceeded on its way through the night. It was a slightly circuitous route to Wembley, through Canterbury, Charing, Maidstone, Westerham, Redhill, Reigate, Dorking, Guildford, Bagshot, Ascot, Windsor, Slough and Uxbridge.

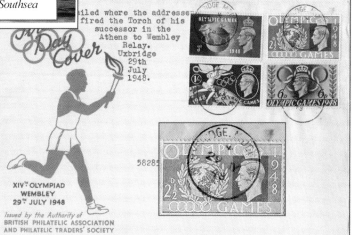

The King declared the Games open, the Olympic Flag being carried round the track, to be flown throughout the Games.

(1948 maximum-card; St. Kitts, 2011 stamp from miniature sheet [enlarged]).

Sigfrid Edstrom, President of the International Olympic Committee, handed the Olympic Flag to the Lord Mayor of London.

(Topps trading card 2012)

Up Olympic Way the crowds delayed the passage, and the Torch arrived just 30 seconds behind schedule for the final lap during the Opening Ceremony, when the athlete John Mark lit the Olympic Cauldron.

Topps trading card 2012

Time Out postcard 2012

Spectator's postcard-sized photograph

Coca Cola postcard, Atlanta 1996

Isle of Man stamp, 2004

At 9am on Sunday 1st August Lord Burghley lit a Torch from the Olympic Flame, and it was carried day and night through Uxbridge, Slough, Maidenhead, Reading, Basingstoke, Andover, Salisbury, Sherbourne, Yeovil, Exeter and Newton Abbott, to arrive in Torquay where the Flame was lit at Torre Abbey at 11am on 2nd August.

Olympic torch handover, Cemetery Junction, Reading
1st August, 1948
Reading Museum (Reading Borough Council)

historyp|n

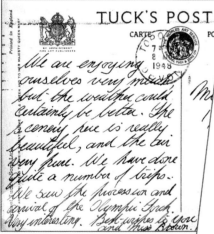

We are enjoying ourselves very much but the weather could certainly be better. The scenery here is really beautiful, and the air very pure. We have done quite a number of trips. We saw the procession and carnival of the Olympic Torch. Very interesting. Best wishes to you and Miss Bowen.

Letter of thanks from Commander Collins, the Torch Relay organiser, to one of his assistants

PATRON: HIS MAJESTY THE KING.

TELEGRAMS ATHLYMPIC, SOWEST, LONDON
CABLES   ATHLYMPIC, LONDON.

THE ORGANISING COMMITTEE FOR THE XIVᵗʰ OLYMPIAD
LONDON 1948

CITIUS·ALTIUS·FORTIUS

TELEPHONE
MAYFAIR 8882.

DIRECTOR OF ORGANISATION
E. J. HOLT, O.B.E.

PRESIDENT OF THE GAMES
THE RT. HON. VISCOUNT PORTAL, D.S.O. M.V.O.
CHAIRMAN
THE RT. HON. THE LORD BURGHLEY, K.C.M.G.

37, UPPER BROOK STREET,
LONDON, W.1.

GENERAL ORGANISING SECRETARY:
LT. COL. T. P. M. BEVAN, M.C.

FWC/JMW

S. F. Skilton, Esq.,
5, Regina Road,
S. Norwood,
LONDON, S.E.25.

12th August, 1948.

Dear Sidney,

As you will know, the Olympic Torch Relay has been acclaimed as one of the events in the Olympic Festival which, perhaps more than any other, has given expression to the ideals of the Olympic movement. The symbol of the torch, illustrating as it does the efforts of all those who, in these troubled days, are striving for a less anxious life through the closer brotherhood of free and friendly nations, has caught the public imagination in a manner which few people would have believed possible.

There is no doubt that this would not have happened if the organisation had been faulty, while any small mistake would, I am sure, have been picked on by those individuals who always try to find fault with such an event of public interest. The many expressions of pleasure and satisfaction which I have received show that the organisation did not fail, and I wish to send you my very warmest thanks for the great assistance you gave the Organising Committee and for the success of your part in this unusual and at times extremely complicated task.

Yours ever,

Bill Collins

Organiser, Torch Relay.

OLYMPIC GAMES
LONDON 1948

S. F. Skilton, Esq.,
5, Regina Road,
S. Norwood,
LONDON, S.E.25.

From:—THE ORGANISING COMMITTEE FOR THE
XIVth OLYMPIAD, LONDON 1948,
37, UPPER BROOK STREET, LONDON, W.1.

Duplicated letter and instructions from a local organiser to a runner on the Torch Relay to Torquay

OLYMPIC TORCH RELAY

"Blue Ridge,"
31, St. Mark's Ave.,
Salisbury, Wilts.

16th July, 1948.

Dear Sir,

    With reference to the Olympic Torch Relay which is being run on Sunday, August 1st, 1948, accommodation is being provided at the Shaftesbury Grammar School for those who are unable to return to their homes that night.

    Will you kindly let me know by return if you wish accommodation to be reserved for yourself and/or your assistant

    Yours faithfully,

        F. GEO. CHALKE.

    Wiltshire Represent

Postcard-sized photo of a Torch Runner

From F.G. Chalke,
"Blue Ridge,"
31, St. Mark's Ave.,
Salisbury, Wilts.

OLYMPIC TORCH RELAY   Telephone Salisbury 4634.

Runner's Instructions

NAME   Lieut. K.H. Pont

ADDRESS   HMS "Royal Arthur", Corsham.

Your Stage is from   Farm on left at top of Ansty Hill

to   Jeffery's Farm, Donhead

Starting at   10.10   a.m./p.m

Finishing at   10.25   a.m./p.m.

ASSEMBLY POINT: Please be at   The Cafe Rendezvous,

Catherine Street, Salisbury, at 5.0 p.m.

for tea.

xxxxxxxxxxxxxxxxxxxxxxxxxxxxx

WITH YOUR ASSISTANT

After which/
    Both of you will xxxxx be taken by coach to the start of your stage. Your assistant, with your clothing, will stay there until he is picked up by the coach which will pick you up at the end of your run. You will then both be taken to _____
Shaftesbury
where you should arrive at about 10.30   a.m./p.m.

PLEASE ACKNOWLEDGE RECEIPT AND CONFIRM THAT YOU WILL BE PRESENT.
    Signed   *F Geo Chalke,*

    Wiltshire   County Representative

TORCH RELAY (ENGLAND) COMMITTEE

RUNNER SHOULD WEAR CLUB VESTS, WHITE SHORTS AND, IF POSSIBLE, WHITE SHOES.

1948 Stamp Issues World-wide—
first day and other postmarks

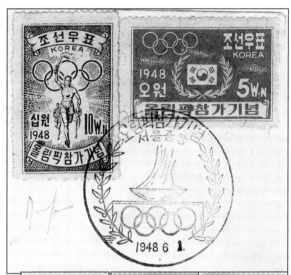

Korea—1 June 1948

5w green — Olympic Rings, Wreath & Korean flag (50,000)

10w violet — Torch runner & rings (*50,000*)

The first day cancel (blue or violet) depicts an Olympic cauldron over the rings.

Monaco—12 July 1948

50c — Athletics (hurdler)
1fr — Athletics (sprinter)
2fr — Discus thrower
2^{f}50 — Basketball
4fr — Swimming
Air-mail
5^f+5 — Rowing
6^f+9 — *Skiing (St. Moritz)*
10^f+15 — Tennis (*not Olympic in 1948*)
15^f+25 — Sailing

(59,975 sets + 500 sets imperf. + de-luxe proofs in 15 colour variants for each stamp + black proofs. There was no special first day cancel)

Discus presentation- proof—black print (50%)

Peru—29 July 1948

1s   Map: Lima-London
2s   Basketball
5s   Discus thrower
10s   Shooting

(30,000 sets plus 8,000 miniature sheets surcharged 2s. for a Children's Hospital)

The 3 higher values are known without the red 'AERO' surcharge.

The 'First Day postmark' appears to be a post office cachet, the stamps being cancelled by a circular date stamp. It can be found in violet, blue, or black, and can be found on covers without the Olympic stamps.

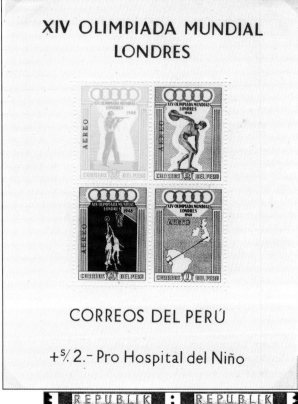

Austria—16 January 1948

Short stamp variety

1s + 50g   Olympic Cauldron

(1,000,000 plus 500 black-print publicity proofs)

The stamp commemorated both the Winter and Summer Games, and had a surcharge for Olympic funds (see also publicity postcards). There was no Olympic first day postmark, but a handstamp on 4 July for Austrian Olympic Day (black or violet).

Postal Stationery—
pre-paid postal cards

Austria

Postal stationery fund-raising card issued by the Austrian Olympic Committee, with pre-printed stamp in the same design as the adhesive.

Japan

As a consequence of the Second World War, Germany and Japan were not invited to participate in the Games. An unusual Japanese postal stationery card depicting the official poster referred to their exclusion, and the fact that they could still see the Games on the news, in newspapers and in the movies. The card advertised 'Heltus D' energy tablets and syrup made by the Dai Nihon Seiyaku Company.

United States

Hollywood's Newsreel Theatre advertising card

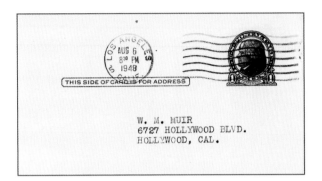

Artcraft First Day Cover advertising card

Postmark Appeal—Finland

Roller cancels "Support the Olympic Appeal" were used in a dozen towns in Finland. In most towns the slogan was just in Finnish, but in Helsinki, Turku and Vasa/Vaasa the text was also in Swedish. The Helsinki single-ring roller is common, the double-ring and all others are scarce or rare. Combination covers are known with Olympic roller cancel from one town, and Olympic roller from another town as an arrival marker on reverse.

1.	Helsinki	6.	Lahti
	a) single ring	7.	Lappeenranta
	b) double ring	8.	Oulu
2.	Jyväskylä	9.	Pori
	a) single ring	10.	Tampere
	b) double ring	11.	Turku Åbo
3.	Kemi	12.	Vaasa
4.	Kotka		
5.	Kuopio		

1. Helsinki single ring, & rare double ring roller (7 May—16 August 1948) (single ring daters known inverted 22 May)

2. Jyväskylä, single ring & double ring varieties (19 May—13 August 1948).

3. Kemi (18 May—22 July 1948)

4. Kotka, (20 May—14 August 1948), here as arrival marker on reverse of a cover with Helsinki roller.

5. Kuopio (18 May—4 September 1948)

6. Lahti (21 May—18 September 1948)

6. Lapeenranta (24 May—1 October 1948)

7. Oulu (19 May—14 August 1948)

8. Pori (13 May—12 August 1948)

10. Tampere (11 May—22 August 1948)

11. Turku Åbo (10 May—18 August 1948)

12. Vasa/Vaasa (15 May 1948—1 April 1949)

Note the extended period of use of this roller slogan.

Olympians Commemorated on Stamps

and on postmarks, postal stationery and postage meters

This chapter lists stamps and other philatelic items that depict or commemorate, directly or indirectly, 1948 Olympic medal winners and competitors and their performances. Stamps are mostly reproduced at slightly less than actual size, other items generally at 70% of actual. Stamps whose postal status is doubtful are listed in dark grey italics, and the stamps are shown at reduced size and framed in red.

Akar, Nasu—Turkey
Wrestling (Freestyle)—Bantamweight Gold
Turkey—3 June 1949

One of a set of 4 stamps marking the European Championships in Istanbul at which Akar also won Gold

Bernardo, Joseph—France
Swimming—4 x 200m relay Bronze
France—28 November 1953

This stamp depicts a relay change-over and is one of a set commemorating French successes at Helsinki in 1952. The French team again won Bronze in the 4 x 200m relay. Joseph Bernardo was the only one of the four who was also in the 1948 team.

Berntsen, Ole—Denmark
Yachting—Dragon Class Bronze
Panama—28 December 1964
(the stamp exists perf. & imperf.)

The stamp commemorated Denmark's Dragon Class Gold in Tokyo in 1964. Ole Berntsen was captain in 1964, and a crew member in 1948 when the Danish yacht 'Snap' took Bronze behind Sweden and Norway.

Blankers-Koen, Fanny—Netherlands
Athletics—   100m Gold
                 200m Gold
                 80m Hurdles Gold
                 4 x 100m Relay Gold

Every Olympic Games produces a star, and in 1948 it was Fanny Blankers-Koen, 'the Flying Dutchwoman' who won 4 Gold medals in the sprints. In the 100m and 200m she comfortably beat Britons into second place, but in the 80m hurdles secured her victory by a nose. Her 4th medal was in the 4 x 100m relay. She took over in 4th place for the final leg but sprinted past Joyce King of Australia to secure Gold.

Netherlands—27 April 2010

The stamp is one of 6 se-tenant in a sheetlet of personalities in the Dutch Summer Stamps series.

Blankers-Koen, Fanny
Dominican Republic—24 January 1957

*This stamp comes from sheets or se-tenant miniature
sheets, perf. & imperf.*
Various proofs or missing colours exist.
*It was overprinted later in 1957 for Hungarian Refugees
and in 1959 for the Pan-American Games*

Missing red & blue

Guyana, 12 August 1991

*The centre stamp in a se-tenant miniature sheet of nine Olympic
medallists (1908, 1948, 1968) issued as one of a series for Barcelona
'92*

Mongolia, 25 March 1969

Fanny Blankers-Koen hurdling.

Guyana, 1996

*From a miniature sheet of 9 stamps showing female Olympic
medallists*
issued for the 1996 games in Atlanta.

Maldives, 1996

*From a se-tenant miniature sheet commemorating female track
and field medal winners*

Palau, 1996

*Se-tenant with a stamp marking Bob Matthias' Decathlon
Gold in 1948 (and 1952)*

Isle of Man, 1 July 2004

*The stamp shows Fanny Blankers-Koen beating Britain's
Maureen Gardner in the 80m hurdles.*

St. Kitts, 14 November 2011

*Fanny Blankers-Koen clasping hands with Maureen
Gardner . (Illustration p.9)*

***Stamps from Apeldoorn, Sharjah,
Khor Fakkan—**see addendum*

Brzac, Jan— Czechoslovakia
Canoe—Canadian Pairs 1km, Gold

Jan Brzac ("Felix"), paired with Bohumil Kudrna, won Gold in London, and Silver in Helsinki in 1952. He had previously won Gold in 1936, paired with Vladimír Syrovátka.

Czech Republic 2007

Commemorative postmark and privately overprinted postal stationery card.

Cabrera Gómez, Delfo—Argentina
Athletics—Marathon, Gold

The finish of the 1948 marathon was almost as dramatic as that in London in 1908. Running in his first marathon, Cabrera held the lead with 5,000 metres to go. Some 600 metres from the stadium he was passed by Etienne Gailly of Belgium, but when he entered the stadium the exhausted Gailly was barely able to stagger round the track. He was easily overhauled by Cabrera, then Britain's Thomas Richards, before gaining a well-earned bronze medal.

Argentina, 16 July 1995

A handstamp in support of Buenos Aires candidature for the 2004 Games, together with a vignette in similar design.

Haiti, 16 May 1969

One of a set depicting marathon winners with a host country stamp in the background (usually found cto)

Grenada, 1996

One of a se-tenant sheetlet of 9 marathon winner stamps.

Cabrera Gómez, Delfo
Argentina, 2009

Miniature sheet

Cam, Edwin Vasquez—Peru
Shooting—   Free Pistol (50m) Gold

Cam's medal is Peru's first and only Olympic Gold Medal

Peru, 2008

Capilla Perez, Joaquin—Mexico
Diving—   Platform   Bronze
                Springboard 4th

Dominican Republic, 12 November 1957

*The stamp commemorates his Gold medal in Platform Diving at
Melbourne in 1956. He also won a Bronze in 1956 on the Springboard, and
Silver in Helsinki in 1952 (Platform).*
*The stamp comes in tête-bêche pairs, perf. and imperf. and in a se-tenant miniature sheet, also perf.
and imperf. It was overprinted in 1958 with a 2c surcharge plus a Star of David or Red Crescent, for
UN Relief of Palestinian Refugees.*

Cevona, Václav— Czechoslovakia
Athletics—1500m 4th

He competed again in the 1952 Olympics but did not reach the final.

Czech Republic, 15 October 2005

Commemorative meter and privately overprinted postal stationery card.

Chychla, Zygmunt—Poland
Boxing—Welterweight 5th

Chychla only reached the quarter-final in 1948, but took Gold at Helsinki in 1952, on the way beating Julius Torma of Czechoslovakia who had taken Gold in 1948.

Poland, 15 June 1960

Issued in a se-tenant block of 4 to mark Chychla's Helsinki Gold (perf. and imperf),

Cia, Maurio—Argentina
Boxing—Light-heavyweight Bronze
Argentina, 10 August 1998

Handstamp from Buenos Aires marking all Argentine medals of 1948

Claudius, Leslie—India
Hockey Team Gold
Dominican Republic, 30 October 1958

The stamp celebrates India's 1956 Gold in hockey; Leslie Claudius was a member of that team (but is not identified as depicted on the stamp). He did not play in the 1948 Final.

It exists perf. and imperf. and in a se-tenant miniature sheet; there is also an International Geophysical Year overprint.

Consolini, Adolfo—Italy
Athletics—Discus, Gold

Consolini also won Silver in Helsinki. In 1960 he took the Olympic Oath on behalf of the athletes.

Italy: 7 May 2000

Handstamp for the 30th Anniversary of the foundation of the Adolfo Consolini Sporting Group, and 29th Anniversary of the Cermenate Philatelic Society.

11 September 2010

Handstamp for the exhibition 'Friulhobby' in Mortegliano

***Mahra: 1968** perf & imperf (with orange border)*

Davis, John—USA
Weightlifting—Heavyweight, Gold

Davis also took Gold in 1952

Equatorial Guinea, 1972

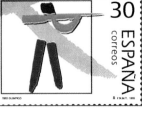

De Almeida Bello, Duarte Manuel Pinto Coelho—Portugal
Yachting—Swallow Class, Silver

De Almeida Bello was helmsman, with his brother Fernando Pinto Coelho Bello. [*The names use the format of the Official Report; they may be set out differently in other sources*]

Portugal, 2008

The stamp is from a presentation booklet issued by the Portuguese Post Office (CTT) "Portugal Nos Jogos olimpicos 1912-2008", with 24 different stamps, self-adhesive in Portuguese personalised stamp format, and several pages of descriptive text; 7,500 copies (available from post offices)

De Gozalo, Angel Leon—Spain
Shooting—Free Pistol (50m), 6th

Spain, 2 June 1995

Stamp from a Se-tenant sheetlet marking Spain's Olympic Silver Medallists.

Paraguay, 5 January 1989

From se-tenant sheetlet marking Barcelona's candidature for 1992 (with candidature logo)

De Pietro, Joseph—USA
Weightlifting—Bantamweight, Gold

Grenada, 1996

From a se-tenant miniature sheet honouring nine different weight-lifters.

Dillard, William Harrison—USA
Athletics—   100m   Gold
4 x 100m relay Gold

A hurdler rather than a sprinter, Dillard failed to qualify for the 110m hurdles in 1948. He went on to take Gold in that event in 1952, as well as Gold again in the 4 x 100m relay.

Guyana, 12 August 1991

The stamp honours his 100m win, and is from a se-tenant sheetlet of nine.

Doğu, Yaşar —Turkey
Wrestling, Freestyle—Welterweight, Gold

Turkey—3 June 1949

One of a set of 4 stamps marking the European Championships in Istanbul at which Doğu also won Gold, but at Middleweight.

D'Oriola, Christian—*see addendum*

Douglas, Herb—USA
Athletics—Long Jump, Bronze

USA, 17 April 1993

Handstamp for Wilkpex '93 in Wilkinsburg, Pennsylvania—on a cover signed by Herb Douglas

Dupont, Jacques—France
Cycling—1km Time-trial, Gold
France, 2004/5

Post paid envelope (PAP in France) ponsored by the local authority in Lézat (Southern France) from where Jacques Dupont emanates.

el Touni, Khadr—Egypt
Weightlifting—Middleweight, 4th

El Touni won Middleweight Gold in 1936, lifting 15 kg more than the Heavyweight Gold Medallist. In 1948 he fell ill the night before the Games. Competing in considerable pain, he lost the Bronze Medal on a tie-break, and was then rushed straight to hospital for surgery.

Egypt, 1 June 2002

The stamp is se-tenant with one for Ibrahim Shams (see below)

Elvstrøm, Paul Bert—Denmark
Yachting—Firefly (Finn) Class, Gold

Elvstrøm repeated his success in 1952, 1956, and 1960, becoming one of only a handful of Olympians to have won four consecutive Gold Medals. He continued competing until 1988, sailing Tornado Class catamarans with his daughter Inge Trine Elvstrøm. (In 1988, at the age of 60, he was 15th. In 1996 he was declared "Danish Sportsman of the Century.

Guyana, 12 August 1991

From a se-tenant sheetlet of 9 1908, 1948 and 1968 medal winners.

Francis, Ranganandhan—India
Hockey Team Gold
Dominican Republic, 30 October 1958

The stamp celebrates India's 1956 Gold in hockey; Francis was a member of that team (but is not identified as depicted on the stamp).

It exists perf. and imperf. and in a se-tenant miniature sheet; there is also an International Geophysical Year overprint.

François, Atilio—Uruguay
Cycling—Team Pursuit, 4000m, 4th
Uruguay, 29 November 1997

The stamp celebrates his becoming cycling World Vice-Champion in Paris in 1947. It comes in a se-tenant vertical strip of five sportsmen

Fredriksson, Gert Fridolf—Sweden
Canoe—   Kayak Singles 1km, Gold
Kayak Singles 10km, Gold

Fredriksson won the K1 1000m Gold in 1952, and repeated the double in 1956. In 1960 he won K2 Gold with Sven-Olov Sjödelius, bringing his tally to six Olympic Golds. He also won a Silver in Helsinki and a Bronze in Rome. In 1956, Fredriksson was awarded the Mohammed Taher Trophy by the IOC, for his contributions to canoeing.

Sweden 21 May 1992

Issued se-tenant in a 'Swedish Gold' booklet

Guyana, 12 August 1991

From a se-tenant sheetlet of nine 1908, 1948 and 1968 winners.

Gallardo, César—Uruguay
Fencing—Foil (Team—Captain), 2nd Round
Uruguay, 16 August 2002

Gardner, Maureen—Great Britain
Athletics—   80m hurdles, Silver
4 x 100m relay, 4th
Isle of Man, 1 July 2004

The stamp shows her being beaten by Fanny Blankers-Koen (on her left) in the 80m hurdles.

St. Kitts, 14 November 2011

Maureen Gardner clasping hands with Fanny Blankers-Koen (from miniature sheet).

Gerevich, Aladár—Hungary
Fencing—Sabre (Individual), Gold
Sabre (Team), Gold

Named 'the Greatest Olympic swordsman ever', Gerevich won
Gold in 1932, 1936, 1948, 1952, 1956 and 1960, six
consecutive Sabre Team Golds, plus just the one
individual gold in 1948. He also won a
Silver and two Bronzes.

Hungary, 26 May 1952

Hungary, 25 Sept. 1956

Hungary, 27 April 1992

*Pre-stamped postcard (portrait 'stamp') and
first day postmark.*

Hungary, 10 Dec. 2010

*Miniature sheet for the
50th Anniversary of the Rome
Olympics includes Gerevich
in the border.*

Hungary, 13 Nov. 2010

*Handstamp for his birth
centenary.*

Guyana, 12 Aug. 1991

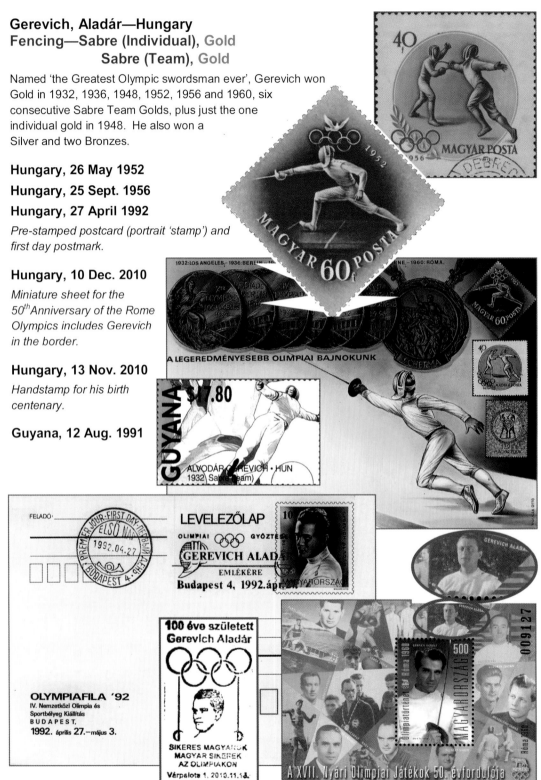

Gren, Gunnar—Sweden
Football—Gold

Gren played for IFK Gothenberg, and AC Milan, where he was one of the "Gre-No-Li" trio of forwards (Gren, Nordahl and Liedholm).

San Marino, 20 September 1999

From a miniature sheet marking the Centenary of AC Milan

Grönberg, Axel
Wrestling—Greco-Roman, Middleweight, Gold
Turkey—3 June 1949

One of a set of 4 stamps marking the European Championships in Istanbul at which he also won Gold.

Gyarmati, Deszö—Hungary
Water Polo—Team, Silver

Hungary, 20 February 1965

The stamp commemorates the team Gold in Tokyo in 1964, at which Gyarmati won his 3rd Gold medal (1952, 1956 and 1964). In 1960 the team secured Bronze.

Holeček, Josef—Czechoslovakia
Canoe—Canadian Singles, 1000m—Gold

Holeček also won Gold in the same event in Helsinki 1952.

Czech Republic, 16 November 2002

Meter and privately overprinted postal card

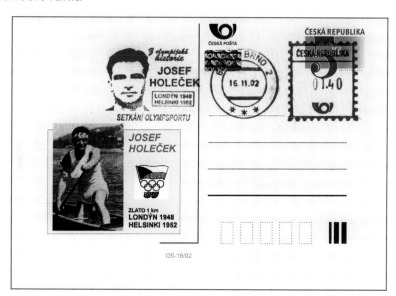

Iglesias, Rafael—Argentina
Boxing—Heavyweight, Gold

Argentina, 10 August 1998

Handstamp marking the 50th Anniversary of the London Games, and all Argentine medals.

Jany, Alexandre—France
Swimming— 100m freestyle 5th
            400m freestyle 6th

France—28 November 1953

This stamp depicts a relay change-over and is one of a set commemorating French successes at Helsinki in 1952. The French team won Bronze in the 4 x 200m relay. Alexandre Jany was one of the medal-winning foursome.

Karpati, Rudolf—Hungary
Fencing—Sabre, Team—Gold

Guyana, 12 August 1991

Hungary, 10 December 2010: *The miniature sheet commemorates Hungarian medal successes in the Rome Olympics in 1960. The stamp depicts Karpati. He repeated his 1948 success with another Sabre Team Gold in Helsinki. He won individual and Team Golds in Melbourne in 1956 and Rome in 1960.*

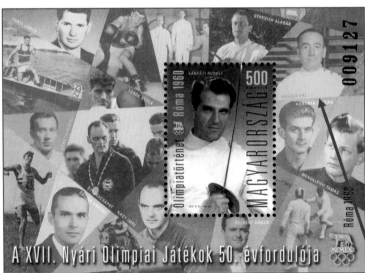

Kovács, Pál—Hungary
Fencing—Sabre, Team—Gold

Kovacs had won Sabre Team Gold in 1936, Team and individual in 1952, Team in 1956 (he was 7th individually) and Team Gold again in 1960

Hungary, 10 December 2010:

Kovacs is depicted in the stamp surround.

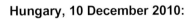

Kovács, Pál—Hungary
Fencing—Sabre,
Team—Gold

Hungary, 28 October 2008

Kovacs is depicted in the stamp surround

Hungary, 26 May 1952

Guyana, 12 August 1991

Laing, Leslie—Jamaica
Athletics— 200m—6th
4x400m—dnf

Jamaica, 21 July 1980

Jamaica, 1984

Both stamps commemorate the 4x400m Gold at Helsinki in 1952. All 4 of that team competed in London in 1948 (Laing, McKenley, Rhoden, Wint)

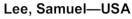

Lee, Samuel—USA
Diving— Platform—Gold
Springboard—Bronze

Tanzania, 18 September 1995

Lee also won platform Gold in 1952. The stamp is from a se-tenant miniature sheet.

Liedholm, Nils— Sweden
Soccer—Team Gold

A renowned midfield player, Liedholm went on to join A.C. Milan in 1949. He formed one of the famous 'Gre-No-Li' trio with Gunnar Gren and Gunnar Nordahl (also in the 1948 Olympic team).

Sweden, 26 March 2004

From a booklet of 6 se-tenant stamps

San Marino, 20 Sept 1999

In a miniature sheet for the Centenary of A.C. Milan

Lombardi, Pietro—Italy
Graeco-Roman Wrestling—Flyweight—Gold

Yemen Arab Republic, 3 December 1971 perf. & imperf. (metallic colour changed)

Lombardio, Adesio—Uruguay
Basketball—Team—5th

Uruguay, 29 November 1997

*The stamp celebrates his participation in the team that won Bronze in Helsinki in 1952.
It comes in a se-tenant vertical strip of five sportsmen*

Lopez Testa, Juan—Uruguay
Athletics— 100m—semi-final
         200m—1st round
         4x100m relay—1st round

Uruguay, 29 November 1997

The stamp commemorates his victory in the 100m. In the South American championships of 1947.

It comes in a se-tenant vertical strip of five sportsmen

Lundberg, Ragnar—Sweden
Athletics—Pole Vault—5th

Sierra Leone, 6 February, 1995

The stamp commemorates his Bronze Medal in Helsinki in 1952.

Mangiarotti, Edoardo—Italy
Fencing— Épée, Individual—Bronze
Épée, Team—Silver
Foil, Team—Silver

1948 was a disappointing year for him—he won Gold in 1936 (team épée), 1952 (individual and team épée), 1956 (team foil and team épée), and 1960 (team épée). He won two more silvers in Helsinki (individual and team foil), and one in Rome (team foil). His second Bronze came in 1956 for individual épée.

Guyana, 12 August 1991,

The stamp commemorates his first Gold Medal in 1936, and comes from a se-tenant sheetlet of nine.

Mathias, Robert Bruce—USA
Athletics—Decathlon—Gold

The youngest Gold medallist in track and field (aged 17) he also won Gold in Helsinki in 1952 (by an incredible 912 points!). In 1966 he was elected to the House of Representatives and served 4 two-year terms.

Dominican Republic, 24 January 1957
(perf. and imperf.)

Tanzania, 18 September 1995

Liberia, 1996

From a se-tenant sheetlet of nine.

Palau, 1996

Se-tenant with a stamp for Fanny Blankers-Koen

St. Vincent 1996

St. Vincent 2008

St Kitts 14 November 2011

(from a se-tenant miniature sheet)

***Paraguay,
23 March 1971***

***Manama, 1971—
see addendum***

McKenley, Herbert "Herb")—Jamaica
Athletics— **400m—Silver**
200m—4th
4x400m relay—dnf

Jamaica, 21 July 1980
Jamaica, 1984

The 1980 stamp commemorates the 4x400m Gold at Helsinki in 1952. All four of that team competed in London in 1948 (Laing, McKenley, Rhoden, Wint)

Mena e Silva, Luis—Portugal
Equestrian—Dressage, team—Bronze
Dressage, individual—12th

His horse was "Fascinante".

Portugal, 2008

Self-adhesive stamp, laser-printed in personalised stamp format ("Meuselo") in a booklet marking all Portuguese Olympic medals (7,500 copies with 24 different stamps @ €19.20, roughly four times face).

Portugal **CTT**   **N**20grs

Mimoun O'Katcha, Alain—France
Athletics—10,000m—Silver

Mimoun won silver in the 5,000m and 10,000m in Helsinki in 1952 (behind Emil Zatopek, as in 1948 in the 10,000m), and Gold in the marathon in 1956

France, 28 Nov. 1953

Dominican Republic 18 July 1957

Haiti, 16 May 1969

Grenada, 1996

Yemen Republic, 4 April 1972
Guinea Republic, 16 July 2001
Label se-tenant with de Coubertin stamp.

Guinea Republic, 2007, stamp and miniature sheet—see appendix

Misáková, Eliška—Czechoslovakia
Gymnastics—Team Combined (Women's)

On arrival in London Eliška was taken ill and died of polio on the day her team-mates won the Gold Medal

Czech Republic, 1998, *Slogan postmark*

Muller-Preis, Ellen—Austria
Fencing—Foil—Bronze

Of dual Austrian/German nationality she fenced for Austria, and won Gold in 1932 in the Individual Foil. She won Bronze in Berlin in 1936 (one of a number of Jews competing), and Bronze again in 1948.

Guinea-Bissau, 20 July 1983
Paraguay, 13 June 1983

Nordahl, Gunnar—Sweden
Football—Gold

Gunnar played for IFK Gothenberg, and AC Milan, where he was one of the "Gre-No-Li" trio of forwards (Gren, Nordahl and Liedholm).

San Marino, 20 September 1999

From a miniature sheet marking the Centenary of AC Milan

Paes [Pais], Fernando—Portugal
Equestrian—Dressage, team—Bronze
Dressage, individual—9th

His horse was "Matamás".

Portugal, 2008

Self-adhesive stamp, laser-printed in personalised stamp format ("Meuselo") in a booklet marking all Portuguese Olympic medals (7,500 copies with 24 different stamps @ €19.20, roughly four times face).

Ostermeyer, Micheline—France
Athletics—   Shot Put—Gold
Discus—Gold
High Jump—Bronze

Guinea Republic, 2007

Portrait in the margin of a miniature sheet—see entry for Emil Zátopek

---

Papp, László—Hungary
Boxing—Middleweight—Gold

Papp won his first Gold in London, at Middleweight, winning Gold again in 1952 and 1956 at Light-Middleweight.

Mongolia, 25 March 1969

Sierra Leone, 2008 *(from se-tenant m/s)*

Papp, László—Hungary
Hungary, 3 June 2005

Handstamp.

Hungary, 24 March 2006

Miniature Sheet (Melbourne)

Postal card (imprinted stamp of László Papp)

Handstamp, Budapest (80th Anniversary of his birth)

Hungary, 24 October 2008

Papp's 1952 Gold is commemorated on the stamp surround of a miniature sheet

Ajman, 27 Sep.1971

N. Korea, 16 June 1978

Perez, Pascual—Argentina
Boxing—Flyweight—Gold

Argentina, 10 August 1998

Handstamp commemorating all Argentinean medals won in 1948, including two Golds and a Bronze in boxing..

Persson, Erik—Sweden
Wrestling—Freestyle Bantamweight—5th

Turkey—3 June 1949 (SG 1408; Scott 988)

One of a set of 4 stamps marking the European Championships in Istanbul at which Persson is understood to have won Gold

Pinto Coelho Bello, Fernando—Portugal
Yachting—Swallow Class, Silver

Fernando crewed for his brother, Duarte Manuel De Almeida Bello. [*The names use the format of the Official Report; they may be set out differently in other sources*]

Portugal, 2008

The stamp is from a presentation booklet issued by the Portuguese Post Office (CTT) "Portugal Nos Jogos olimpicos 1912-2008", with 24 different stamps, self-adhesive in Portuguese personalised stamp format, and several pages of descriptive text; 7,500 copies (available from post offices)

Rautavaara, Kai Tapio—Finland
Athletics—Javelin—Gold

Rautavaara was also an accomplished archer and won Gold with the Finnish team at the 1958 World Championships, but was best known as a popular singer in the 1950s and 1960s and as a film actor.

Central African Republic, 1993

From a se-tenant sheetlet of 9 designs marking the Centenary of the Olympic Games. (Also available as an individual plate proof on matt card)

Rhoden, Vincent George—Jamaica
Athletics—   400m—semi-finals
4 x 400m relay—dnf

He won Gold in both these events in 1952

Jamaica, 21 July 1980

Jamaica, 1984

Risso, Eduardo—Uruguay
Rowing—Single Sculls—Silver

Risso also competed in the 1952 Olympics

Uruguay, 1 October 1996

The stamp comes in a se-tenant strip of 5 Uruguayan sportsmen

Ružicková, Véra—Czechoslovakia
Gymnastics—Team Combined (women) - Gold

Czech Republic,
31 March 2007—meter

Sakata, Toshiyuki ("Harold")—USA
Weightlifting—Light-heavyweight—Silver

Born in Hawaii of Japanese parentage he became a professional wrestler under the name "Tosh Togo" , but is best known for his role as 'Oddjob' in the James Bond Goldfinger film.

Grenada, 1996

From a se-tenant miniature sheet of nine Olympic weightlifters.

Savolainen, Heikki—Finland
Gymnastics—   Pommel Horse—Gold
Team—Gold
Parallel Bars—6th
Rings—8th

Savolainen won pommel horse Bronze in 1928, three Bronzes and a Silver in 1932, Team Bronze in Berlin in 1936, and again in Helsinki in 1952.

Finland, 16 April 1945

Shams, Ibrahim—Egypt
Weightlifting—Lightweight—Gold

Shams won Bronze in the Featherweight (under 60 kg) in Berlin in 1936

Egypt, 1 June 2002

Se-tenant with a stamp for Khadr el Touni (q.v.)

Singh, Gurdev—India
Hockey Team—Gold
Dominican Republic, 30 October 1958

The stamp celebrates India's 1956 Gold in hockey; Gurdev Singh Kullar was a member of that team. It exists perf. and imperf. and in a se-tenant miniature sheet; there is also an International Geophysical Year overprint.

Randhir Singh Gentle
Was also a member of both teams but has not been identified on the stamp.

Smith, Owen Guinn—USA
Athletics—Pole Vault—Gold
Maldives, 1996

The text just states 'Pole Vault London 1948'

St. Cyr, Henri Julius Reverenoy—Sweden
Equestrian—Dressage, Individual—5th

He won Golds in the team and individual events in 1952 and 1956, and took the Olympic Oath in Stockholm for the 1956 Equestrian Olympics.

Guyana, 12 August 1991

From a se-tenant miniature sheet of nine.

Stalder, Josef—Switzerland
Gymnastics—Horizontal Bars—Gold
Team—Silver
Parallel Bars—Bronze
All-round—4th
Rings—5th
Pommel Horse—8th

He secured two more Silver and two more Bronze medals in 1952 at Helsinki, and was Swiss Sports Personality of the Year for 1952.

North Korea, 16 June 1978

Strickland, Shirley—Australia
Athletics—4 x 100m Relay—Silver
100m—Bronze
80m Hurdles—Bronze
200m—4th

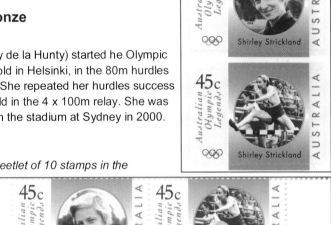

Shirley Barbara Strickland (later Shirley de la Hunty) started he Olympic career in London. She won her first Gold in Helsinki, in the 80m hurdles (and also won a Bronze in the 100m). She repeated her hurdles success in Melbourne in 1956, and added a Gold in the 4 x 100m relay. She was one of the runners carrying the Torch in the stadium at Sydney in 2000.

Australia, 21 January 1998

2 stamps se-tenant horizontally in a sheetlet of 10 stamps in the

Australian Legends series.
Also as a vertical pair, with die-cut perforations, in a self-adhesive booklet of 10 (5 different pairs).
Also a postage-paid maximum card.

The stamps were re-issued in 2007 in a booklet marking ten years of the Australian Legends series, in a pane of four values (the two Shirley Strickland beneath the two for Murray Rose). The stamps are still inscribed '1998' but have distinct shade differences.

Dominican Republic, 12 November 1957

Mali, 13 November 1972

Székely, Èva—Hungary
Swimming—200m Breaststroke—4th
4 x 100m Relay—5th

Èva Székely won Gold in the 200m in Helsinki, but slipped back to Silver in 1956 in Melbourne

Hungary, 28 October 2008

Images on stamp surround of miniature sheet commemorating Hungary's medals in Helsinki in 1952

Takács, Károly—Hungary
Shooting—25m Rapid Pistol—Gold

Takács is the first known physically disabled Olympic competitor—he badly injured his right hand in military training and switched to shooting with his left hand. He repeated his success with a second Gold in Helsinki in 1952.

Hungary, 28 October 2008

Images on stamp surround of miniature sheet commemorating Hungary's medals in Helsinki in 1952

Dominica, 2004

Torma, Július—Czechoslovakia
Boxing—Welterweight—Gold

He competed again, unsuccessfully, in 1952 and 1956

Czechoslovakia, 1-24 June 1998

Handstamp

Valadas, Francisco—Portugal
Equestrian—Dressage, team—Bronze
Dressage, individual—10th

His horse was "Feitiço".

Portugal, 2008

Self-adhesive stamp, laser-printed in personalised stamp format ("Meuselo") in a booklet marking all Portuguese Olympic medals (7,500 copies with 24 different stamps @ €19.20, roughly four times face).

Wilkes, Rodney—Trinidad
Weightlifting—
Featherweight—Silver

Wilkes was the first athlete from Trinidad to win an Olympic medal. He competed again in 1952, securing Bronze, and in 1956 coming 4th.

Trinidad, 7 September 1972

Trinidad, 22 July 1980

Wint, Arthur Stanley—Jamaica
Athletics—400m—Gold
800m—Silver
4 x 400m—dnf

Wint won Gold again in 1952 in the 4 x 400m relay, and another Silver in the 800m

Grenada, 24 September 1968
2c & 50c

The stamps come from se-tenant sheets in a presentation sheet format. They were overprinted with surcharges in 1969.

Jamaica, 1984

Zátopková, Dana—Czechoslovakia
Athletics—Javelin—7th

Wife of Emil Zátopek, she went on to win Gold at Helsinki in 1952, just an hour after Emil won the 5,000 metres. In Rome in 1960 she took the Silver medal.

Czechoslovakia, 15 September 1953

Czechoslovakia, 16 October 1992

Meter, with her husband—*see his entry*

Czech Republic, 25 October 2001

Slogan postmark from Prague, for 80 years of Police Sports

Czech Republic, April 2012

Meter commemorating Czech javelin throwers including Dana Zátopková.

Emil Zátopek—Czechoslovakia
Athletics—10,000m—Gold
5,000m—Silver

One of the most celebrated runners of his generation, he was competing in only his second 10,000m when he won Gold in 1948. In 1952, having taken 5,000m and 10,000m Golds he decided to compete in the marathon, the first he had ever run, and astonishingly secured Gold in an Olympic record time. Injury affected him in 1956, and he could only finish 6th in the marathon.

Czechoslovakia, 24 April 1954

A stamp in a Czech sports series.

Czechoslovakia, 16 April 1965

This stamp specifically celebrates his 1952 victories.

Czechoslovakia, 30 April 1968

Zátopek is the inspiration for the runner on one of the Czech stamps marking the 1968 Mexico Olympics.

Haiti, 16 May 1969

This stamp is mostly found cto.

Guyana 12 August 1991

From a miniature sheet of nine stamps, se-tenant with the stamp for Fanny Blankers-Koen

Maldive Islands, 1996

Another stamp marking his Helsinki victories

Togo, 1996

From a se-tenant miniature sheet of nine, this stamp specifically commemorates his 1948 Gold

Grenada, 1996

From a se-tenant miniature sheet celebrating nine marathon medallists (and marking his 1952 victory)

Sharjah, 15 October 1968;
Khor Fakkan 1969

The Khor Fakkan 'stamp' is an overprint of that from Sharjah.

Olympians Commemorated

Emil Zátopek—Czechoslovakia
Athletics—10,000m—Gold
5,000m—Silver

**Czechoslovakia,
31 May 1989**

*Postal stationery
envelope. The text
translates:*

*"IOC President
J. A. Samaranch
presented the Olympic
Order on 31 May 1989 to
Honoured Master of
Sports Emil Zátopek"*

*He received the Pierre de
Coubertin medal
posthumously in
December 2000.*

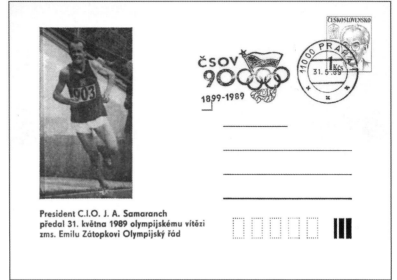

Czech Republic, 19 May 1999

a. *Postal stationery card for the
Centenary of the Czech
Olympic Committee, depicting
Zatopek.*

b. *Postmark from Prague for
'Olympsport 99' reproducing
the 1954 Czech stamp.*

Czechoslovakia, 1992

*Meter celebrating the 70th
birthdays of Dana and Emil
Zátopek (both 19.9.1922) &
meeting of the Czech
Olympic Club at the Hotel
International, Prague
(card signed by Dana
Zátopková)*

Emil Zátopek—Czechoslovakia

Czech Republic, November-December 2000

a. *Meter from the Czech Olympic Committee in Prague marking the death of Zátopek on 21 November 2000 (earliest date seen 24.11.00)*

b. *Postal stationery card*

Czech Republic, 24 June 2001

a. *Postal stationery envelope (with cachet in Gold or in Silver)*

b. *Memorial postmark (machine strike or hand-stamp)*

Both commemorate the unveiling on 24 June 2001 of the memorial stone on Zátopek's grave at Rožnov pod Radhoštěm

27 July 2002

The handstamp was reused at Rožnov pod Radhoštěm Museum to mark the 50th anniversary of his victories in Helsinki, and

19 September 2002 *to mark the 80th anniversary of his birth. A postal stationery card was also issued with cachet recording his Helsinki victories.*

Emil Zátopek—Czechoslovakia

Emil Zátopek was born in Kopřivnice in Moravia. On 30 November 2000, 8 days after his death, Zátopek was unanimously voted "Czech Sporting Legend of the Twentieth Century."

Czech Republic, 11 September 2002

A stamp to honour the Czech Sporting Legend, with first day postmark from his birth-town of Kopřivnice.

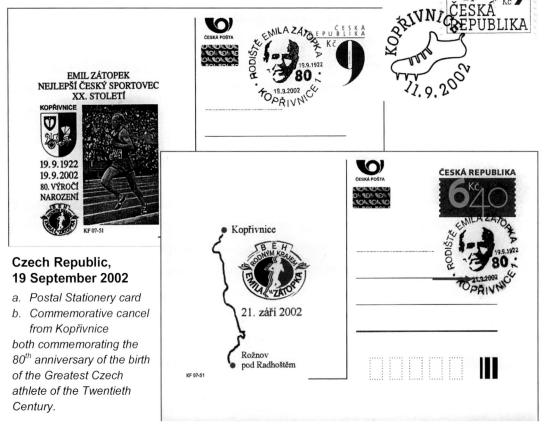

Czech Republic, 19 September 2002

a. Postal Stationery card
b. Commemorative cancel from Kopřivnice
both commemorating the 80th anniversary of the birth of the Greatest Czech athlete of the Twentieth Century.

Czech Republic, 21 September 2002

a. Postal Stationery card
b. Commemorative cancel from Kopřivnice
both commemorating the unveiling of a memorial to Emil Zátopek in Kopřivnice and the inaugural Emil Zátopek Memorial Race from Kopřivnice to Rožnov pod Radhoštěm (which was started by Dana Zátopková, and which has been run annually since.

Yemen Arab Republic, 22 December 1968

The stamp shows the arms of London and Helsinki, and the text over the Olympic Rings reads "E. ZATOPEK CZECHOSLOVAKIA / 5,000m - 10,000m / 1952". It comes perf. and imperf. on white or light-blue paper. The stamp is also known without the text over the rings.

Emil Zátopek—Czechoslovakia

Great Britain, 17 May 2007

A commemorative sheet for the Opening of the new Wembley Stadium included 20 first class stamps (lion and shield) with se-tenant vignettes, including one depicting Emil Zátopek [with a heavy screen], and one recording his 1948 victory. The initial print had a spelling mistake, 'Emile' for 'Emil'. This was spotted and rectified, but a few sheets with the error have reached the market.

Guinea Republic, 16 July 2001

Label se-tenant with de Coubertin stamp. (Only seen as part of a Dutch 'collection', mint or on a maximum card)

Guinea Republic, 2007

Miniature sheet, stamp commemorating his 1948 win in the 10,000 metres.

*In the margin is a portrait of **Micheline Ostermeyer**, Gold Medallist in the discus)*

Addendum

Blankers-Koen, Fanny—Netherlands

Apeldoorn Town post, 1972

Sharjah, 15 Oct. 1968
(perf. imperf. & block)

Khor Fakkan, 1969

Khor Fakkan overprint on the Sharjah stamp and block

D'Oriola, Christian—France
Fencing— Team Foil— Gold
Individual Foil—Silver

D'Oriola won two more foil Golds at Helsinki, and Individual Gold and Team Silver at Melbourne. He was named as "The Fencer of the Twentieth Century" by the International Fencing Federation.

France, 28 Nov. 1953

Sharjah, 15 Oct. 1968
(perf. imperf. & block)

Khor Fakkan, 1969

Khor Fakkan overprint on the Sharjah stamp and block

Mathias, Robert Bruce—USA
Tulare, California, 29-30 July 1950

Commemorative cover for AAU Championships.

Manama, 1971

(perf. imperf. & block)

Mimoun O'Katcha, Alain—France

Yemen Arab Republic, 4 April 1972

Stamp perforated (with blue-grey surround, and imperforate with light-blue surround. The caption on both stamps for Mimoun refers, interestingly to "Stockholm 1956"!

Guinea Republic, 2007—stamp & miniature sheet

Nordahl, Gunnar—Sweden

A pre-stamped postcard commemorating a Football exhibition in the Swedish Postmuseum in Stockholm refers to the fact that Gunnar Nordahl was present at the opening ceremony.

Hungarian Medallists
22 October 2012

*A block celebrating Hungarian 1948 medallists has been announced. Details are not known at the date of going to press, but Gold Medallists were **Gyula Bóbis, Tibor Csik, Ilona Elek, Aladar Gerevich, Olga Gyarmati, Rudolf Karpati, Pal Kovaks, Imre Németh, Laszlo Papp, Ferenc Pataki,** and the **Mens Sabre Team (fencing).***

Other Commemorative Stamps—
Officials, Poster, Torch, Stadium etc

This section includes stamps with a generic Olympic image and caption '1948'. These come from series that chronicle the four year Olympic calendar. There may be additional stamps of this type, especially from 'back-of-the-book' issues that are not illustrated in catalogues, and not listed here.

J. Sigfrid Edström
President of the International Olympic Committee 1946—1952

Born in Sweden, Edström was on the Organising Committee of the 1912 Olympics at Stockholm, and first President of the IAAF. He became an IOC member in 1920, and was acting President from 1942.

San Marino—17 May 1959

One of a series depicting Olympic Presidents

Palau—2004

Romania—1996

Postal-stationery envelope, the stamp indicium depicting the Romanian Olympic Committee logo.

Edström, 1942-1952

PALAU 80¢

CENTENARUL JOCURILOR OLIMPICE
1896 - 1996

SIGFRID EDSTRÖM
Preşedinte C.I.O. 1946 - 1952

ROMÂNIA

ROMÂNIA

150ᴸ

Destinatar _____

_____

Strada _____ Nr. _____

Blocul ____ Scara ____ Etajul ____ Apart. ____

Sector _____ Judeţul _____

Codul	Localitatea

David George Brownlow Cecil,
6th Marquis of Exeter, KCMC, Lord Burghley
Chairman of the 1948 Olympic Organising Committee

Burghley competed in the 1924 Olympics, won Gold in Amsterdam in 1928, in the 400m hurdles, and Silver in Los Angeles in 1932, as a member of the 4x400m relay team. In 1933 he became a member of the IOC. In 1936 he was elected President of the Amateur Athletic Association, and also of the British Olympic Association. In 1946 he became President of the IAAF, and Chairman of the 1948 Olympic Organising Committee. From 1952-1966 he was Vice-President of the IOC.

Dominican Republic—24 January 1957
Perf. & imperf., from sheets, and from se-tenant miniature sheets.

REPUBLICA DOMINICANA

CORREOS 5¢

1928 - LORD BURGHLEY

Wembley Stadium

The Stadium was built for the 1924 British Empire Exhibition, and became Britain's national football stadium. In 1948 it was the venue for the opening Ceremony, and hosted the Athletics, the semi-finals and finals of the football and the hockey, and the equestrian Prix des Nations and Closing Ceremony. Gymnastics was to have been held there, but bad weather flooded the field and so gymnastics was transferred to the Empress Hall at Earl's Court. It closed in October 2000, was demolished in 2003, and a new stadium on the same site was opened in 2007. The new stadium is a soccer venue in 2012.

Nevis—2000
From a se-tenant miniature sheet

Great Britain—1999

A stamp in the Millennium series

NB: there is no other British stamp depicting the old stadium, but a label from a 2007 Commemorative sheet 'Memories of Wembley' shows the stadium. Another Commemorative Sheet has vignettes showing scenes from the World Cup Final of 1966. There are also numerous post-marks, mostly soccer-related, such as the one illustrated here. A full listing is beyond the scope of this hand-book.

St Kitts—2011

A view from the Opening Ceremony

From a se-tenant miniature sheet.

The Torch Relay

Isle of Man—2004

The stamp depicts John Mark, the last Torch Runner, on the Wembley track prior to lighting the Flame in the Cauldron. Note that he is carrying the unique Torch of a special design used exclusively to light the Flame.

Palau—1996

The stamp also includes the London 1948 Emblem, and is se-tenant with a stamp depicting a view at Olympia, with flags including the Union Jack.

The Olympic Poster

Cook Islands—1984

One of a set recalling previous Olympic Games through posters, issued to mark the 1984 Los Angeles Olympics.

Central African Republic 1985

From Olymphilex '85 set

St. Kitts—2011

From a se-tenant miniature sheet.

Fujeira—1972

(Stamp also shows Winston Churchill)

The Olympic Medal

Paraguay—25 November 1972

One of a pair of blocks depicting Olympic medals, this block showing 1936-1972.

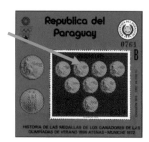

Umm Al Qiwain-1972

As Fujeira, this stamp is se-tenant with stamps depicting posters from other Games. It was issued in two sizes.

Paraguay—22 May 1972

One of a set of 6 blocks depicting Summer and Winter Olympic posters. Only one poster in each block is perforated, in this instance Paris 1924.

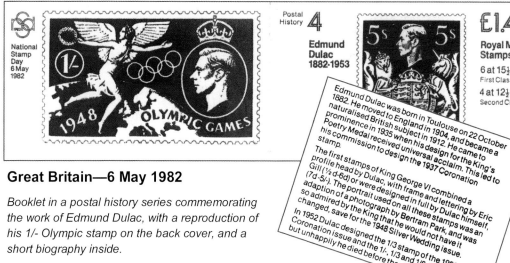

Great Britain—6 May 1982

Booklet in a postal history series commemorating the work of Edmund Dulac, with a reproduction of his 1/- Olympic stamp on the back cover, and a short biography inside.

Edmund Dulac was born in Toulouse on 22 October 1882. He moved to England in 1904, and became a naturalised British subject in 1912. He came to prominence in 1935 when his design for the King's Poetry Medal received universal acclaim. This led to his commission to design the 1937 Coronation stamp.

The first stamps of King George VI combined a profile head by Dulac, with frame and lettering by Eric Gill (½ d-6d) or were designed in full by Dulac himself, (7d -5/-). The portrait used on all these stamps was an adaption of a photograph by Bertram Park, and was so admired by the King that he would not have it changed, save for the 1948 Silver Wedding issue.

In 1952 Dulac designed the 1/3 stamp of the 1953 Coronation issue and the 1/-, 1/3 and 1/6 definitives but unhappily he died before they were issued.

Japan—November 2005

Handstamp marking the award of the 2012 Games to London, with an illustration of the 6D stamp (it is not clear if this is a PO cancel or a cachet).

Germany—31 March 2012

Handstamp from the 13th International Collector's Fair - 30-31 March 2012, German Sports & Olympic Museum, Cologne (commemorating the London 2012 Olympics)

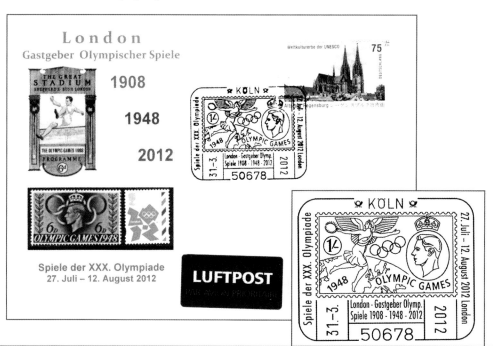

Great Britain—2008: *Commemorative Sheet (A.G. Bradbury [BFDC Ltd History of Britain Sheet No. 26) with images of 1948 stamps and FDCs linked to British Union Flag stamps.*

18 October 1988	**29 September 2001**	**5 August 2005**
Handstamp for National Postal Museum Olympic Exhibition depicts Mercury from the 1/- stamp	*Cancel for the joint meeting of the Society of Olympic Collectors and the French sports collectors' society, AFCOS, at Henley.*	*First day handstamp for the issue of the miniature sheet marking London's successful bid to host the 2012 Olympics.*

GB Philatelic Products

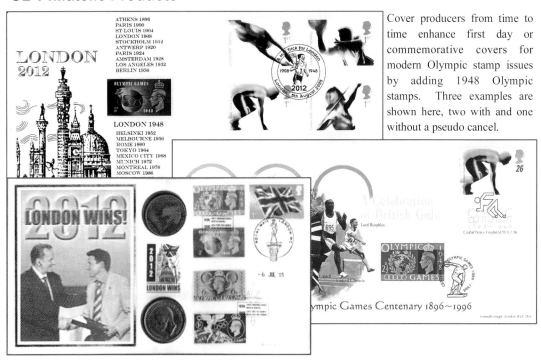

Cover producers from time to time enhance first day or commemorative covers for modern Olympic stamp issues by adding 1948 Olympic stamps. Three examples are shown here, two with and one without a pseudo cancel.

Royal Mail Products 2012—Coin Cover

This was not sold separately but included in a "1948 Heritage Pack" along with a set of the mint stamps, and other non-philatelic ephemera, at a retail price of £69.95. An actual 1948 half-a-crown coin is set into the cover. The stamps, no longer valid for postage, have a pseudo 1948 postmark

Facsimile Pack

A non-postally valid Facsimile Sheet of the four British stamps printed in gravure as a block of four. The pack, written by Douglas Muir, includes details of the selection process and unadopted designs from the 20 invited artists and printers. (Retail £5.95)

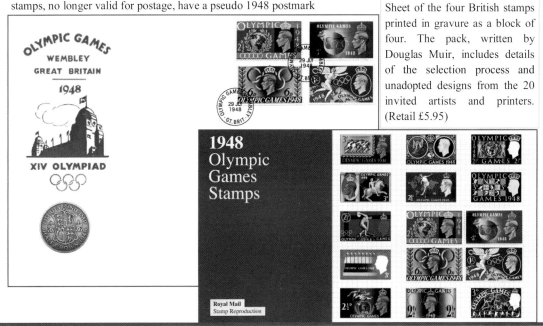

Emblem & Torch
China—2008 'P' stamps

From a series of personalised stamps depicting emblems or logos, and torches, and usually found on commemorative covers.

Stamp on stamp

Kyrgszstan—2002

From a set of 3 sheetlets (8 se-tenant stamps plus a central label, each depicting a stamp from or relating to an Olympic Games.

Haiti—16 May 1969

One of a set depicting marathon winners with a host country stamp in the background (usually found cto).

General
Montserrat—1980

From sheets, and se-tenant miniature sheet.

Paraguay—
1 October 1962

The stamp was also issued imperf. with changed colours

The **St. Kitts** miniature sheet, 2011, with stamps showing the Opening Ceremony at Wembley Stadium, Bob Mathias, Fanny Blankers-Koen with Maureen Gardner, and the official poster.

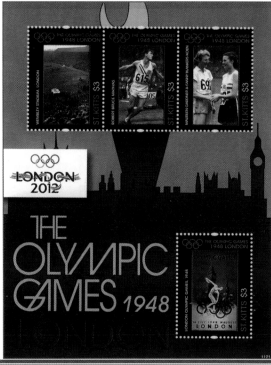

Arab States
Kathiri State in Hadhramaut—1967

Perf. or imperf. in pairs in sheetlets with two stamps for Berlin 1936 and two labels.

Kathiri State of Seiyun (South Arabia), 1966

South Arabia over-printed in green, "London 1948" and rings overprinted in red or black.

Sharjah—10 October 1968; Khor Fakkan—10 October 1968

Perf., imperf., stamp and block. The Khor Fakkan stamps are overprints on Sharjah stamps.

Yemen Arab Republic—1970

Perf.

Imperf.

Yemen Arab Republic—1972

Stamps commemorating St. Moritz & London 1948, perf. and imperf., with gold or silver name panels at right.

Yemen Kingdom—31 May, 1968

Perf., imperf., stamp and block.

Yemen Kingdom—25 December, 1968

Stamp for EFIMEX Stamp Exhibition (Mexico) incorporates an image of the above stamp.
Perf. and imperf.

Malawi—2012

Appearing as the book went to press, a series of sheetlets included one with illustrations of the 6^d and 1/- stamps. The 'stamps' are of doubtful status.

Postcards

There were no mass-market Olympic postcards produced for sale to the general public. The principal reason it is suggested is the lack of card stock after the Second World War. A card is known for the Henley Olympic Regatta, there is one published for the BBC, and there are some artist designed cards, produced in very small numbers, but otherwise visitors and competitors had to rely on cards produced earlier, including cards originally produced for the British Empire Exhibitions of 1924 and 1925!

The listing that follows therefore includes cards mailed in 1948, often with Olympic messages, to give an indication of what was available. It is unlikely to be a complete listing of such cards. Cards are reproduced at between 50% and 70% of actual size

Some cards were produced overseas. Such cards do not appear to have been generally available to the public, although Austrian cards were made available to competitors, and can be found with Wembley and other Olympic postmarks.

Over the years since 1948 cards have been issued relating back to 1948, and continue to be issued even now. Cards depicting medallists often have only a limited circulation in the country of issue. Those listed here will be just a selection, and the author welcomes details of others (please send to marathon@societyofolympiccollectors.org). There have been many printings around the world of the Olympic poster as a postcard; not all such printings are listed here. A number of original (and reproduction) photographs of postcard size can be found, and a selection of these is included in the chapter on ephemera; they do not have postcard backs and are rarely if ever seen postally used.

1   V. Milich (designer) - continents, sportsmen and heraldic

a) buff card 150 x 101mm   b)   buff back, pink face   c)   on commercial plain postcard, with pre-printed 'POSTCARD' text crossed through (smaller dimensions)

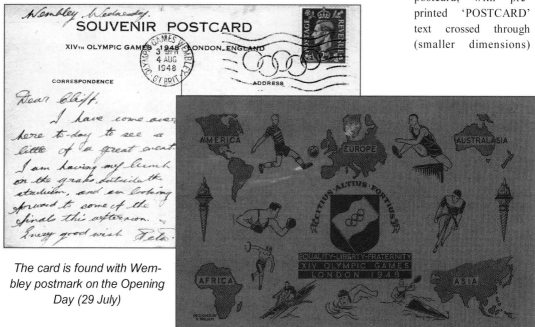

The card is found with Wembley postmark on the Opening Day (29 July)

2 Chariot

3 Greek head

These cards appear to be lino-cuts by the same artist. Neither has a printed postcard back, but both are known mailed from Wembley (14 August)

4 The Henley Royal and Olympic Regatta Course Henley-on-Thames

Photograph by Sport & General, published by J.R. of Henley (no 405). Some copies carry a cachet in purple 'Olympic Games 1948, with compliments from the Citizens of High Wycombe and District'. These cards were presented to rowing competitors being lodged in High Wycombe.

THE HENLEY ROYAL AND OLYMPIC REGATTA COURSE.
HENLEY-ON-THAMES.

5 BBC Broadcasting Centre

The Broadcasting centre was located in the Palace of Arts erected for the British Empire Exhibitions.

The card was printed and published by Waterlow & Sons Ltd, for the BBC.

Wembley

6 Wembley Stadium—
Photochrom 72558

The card illustrated has a Wembley. Middlesex 16 * counter handstamp from the Olympic P.O. in the Civic Hall.

WEMBLEY, THE STADIUM   72558

7 Wembley Stadium—
Photochrom V. 1176

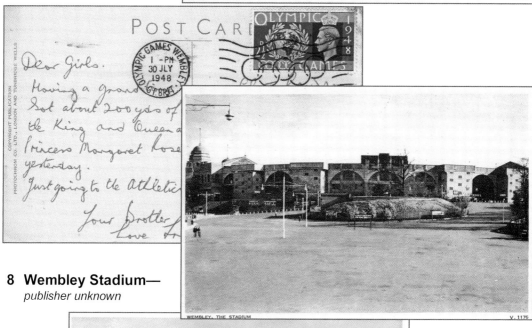

WEMBLEY, THE STADIUM   V. 1176

8 Wembley Stadium—
publisher unknown

WEMBLEY STADIUM

9 The Stadium, Wembley.—(154)
Valentine 227.608JV.

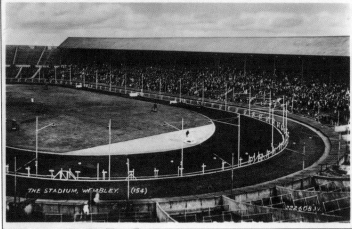

10 Wembley, the Empire Pavilion—
Photochrom V. 1172

The Empire Pavilion housed the Olympic pool, and was venue for the swimming and boxing.

This example, sent from Uxbridge Olympic Village, is signed by members of the Czech gymnastics team.

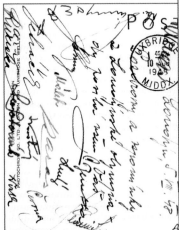

11 Empire Pool & Sports Arena, Wembley (277)
- Valentine G. 1015

12 Empire Pool & Sports Arena, Wembley (274) - Valentine G. 1016

This card shows the pool in recreational use.

13 Empire Pool & Sports Arena, Wembley (275) - Valentine G. 1017

13a Sunbathing Terrace Empire Swimming Pool, Wembley - Valentine G. 1017

14 The Empire Pool & Sports Arena, Wembley - Valentine H. 9219

15 Empire Pool & Stadium, Wembley (23) Photo by Eagle Aerophotos Ltd

Card publisher not stated.

16 Interior Empire Pool. Wembley (20)

Card publisher not stated.

17 Wembley, High Road
Photochrom V. 1175

Mailed during the Games (Olympic slogan postmark)

18 Wembley, High Street
Photochrom V. 1219

Mailed during the Games.

19 Olympic Way, Wembley
40430

This card dates from after the Games.

WD1-6 RAF Camp West Drayton

A series of views of the Camp that became one of the Olympic Villages. These postcards pre-date the Olympics. The camp is believed to have been opened in 1924. Card (2) depicted here was mailed in 1938; none has been reported used during the Olympics.

Olympic Games Box Office—
Acknowledgement card

Illustrated is a card acknowledging a ticket application from an affiliated club. It was mailed (29 January 1948) using the box office meter. Other acknowledgement cards may well exist.

OLYMPIC GAMES BOX OFFICE
Empire Stadium, Wembley

Re National Governing Bodies

Applications (N.G.B.2)

Affiliated Clubs in Great Britain will
not receive details of their allotment
until after 14th February

Bisley

Cards published by Gale & Polden were available to visitors and competitors. Illustrated are cards no. 9 & no. 14, both mailed in July or August 1948.

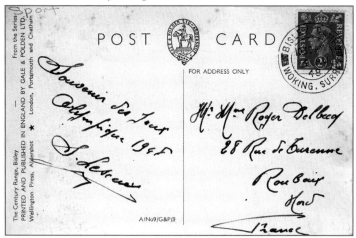

THE CENTURY RANGE, BISLEY   GALE & POLDEN LTD COPYRIGHT

THE CENTURY RANGE, BISLEY   GALE & POLDEN LTD COPYRIGHT

Henley
The Straight Mile, Henley Regatta
T.V.A.P. Oxford, Series III, 1056

Torquay

The Beach, Torbay
Raphael Tuck TQY 398

(for message on this card see the Torch Relay chapter)

Yacht Racing in Torbay
Visick.

Maximum Cards

*Card designed by B.M. Huet, published by
C.M.F. Tyrol-Vorarlberg - I.N.-3-48
It incorporates a cauldron similar to that on
the Austrian stamp.*

Sweden—Stockholm News

*The sports editorial team of Stockholms-
Tidningen rented a house in Oakington [mis-
spelt Oaktington] Avenue Wembley for the
period of the Games and issued this publicity
card with imprinted pseudo-stamp and pseudo
postmark.*

Austria

A set of cards designed by Alfred von Chmielowski was issued by the Austrian Olympic Committee. They were available to competitors and are known used from Wembley and the Olympic Villages.

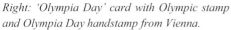

Right: 'Olympia Day' card with Olympic stamp and Olympia Day handstamp from Vienna.

Below: Card sent from West Drayton Olympic Village (West Drayton 6 skeleton)

Czechoslovakia

A series of cards published in support of the Czech Olympic Committee.

Vyddno na podporu československého výboru olympijského

Inter-Continental Swimming Contests—Empire Pool, Wembley

The Olympic competitions finished on the afternoon of 7 August. This postcard, from the Amateur Swimming Association, offered member clubs the opportunity to purchase tickets for this "gala" event in the evening.

SWIMMING CLUBS
HOW TO BOOK SEATS

1. To secure a provisional allocation of tickets, apply as soon as possible, stating the price and the number of seats required. Address your letter to " INTER-CONTINENTAL CONTEST," Box Office, Wembley Stadium Ltd., Wembley. SEND NO MONEY AT THIS STAGE.

2. The Box Office will notify you if your requirements can be filled or, if not, will offer an alternative. A reference number will be quoted with your reservation.

3. Remittances for tickets taken up must then be forwarded not later than Saturday, July 17th, whereupon the tickets will be dispatched to you.
   The reference number must be quoted when sending your Cheque, Money Order, or Postal Order, made payable to Wembley Stadium Ltd. No deposits are accepted.

4. Series tickets and Passes for the Olympic Games are not valid for this Event.

5. Tickets not taken up by July 17th will be released for sale.

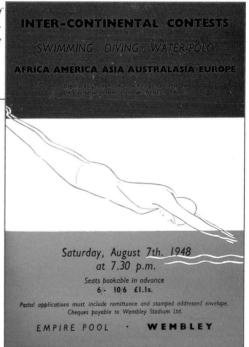

Medallists & Competitors

It is likely that this section is far from complete. Medallists often produce their own publicity cards, and their exploits are commemorated by cards produced in their own country. What follows is just an indicative listing. The chapter on cigarette and collectors' cards includes postcard-sized cards (e.g. the 'Nostalgia' series).

Adam, Pierre—France

Cycling—
4000m Team Pursuit Gold

Other team members were C. Coste, S Blusson, F Decanali

Beyaert, José—France

Cycling—
Individual Road Race Gold
Team Road Race Bronze

A search of the internet suggests that Beyaert had a very colourful life both before and after the 1948 Olympics!

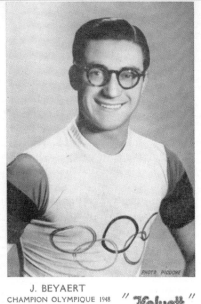

Blankers-Koen, Fanny—Netherlands

100m, 200m, 80m Hurdles, 4 x 100m relay—Gold

It is not clear whether this on the left is a postcard or a photo-card, nor whether it is an original or printed signature.

Card published by the Ouwehands Deer Park, at Rhenen

Caron, Henri—France

Athletics—50km walk, 11th

By his shoulder is a 1948 Olympic banner

Consolini, Adolfo—Italy

Athletics—Discus, Gold

Card issued in homage in 2010

Omaggio a ADOLFO CONSOLINI

d'Oriola, Christian—France
Fencing —   Team Foil Gold;
Individual Foil Silver

D'Oriola won two more Golds at Helsinki, and Individual Gold and Team Silver at Melbourne. He was named as "The Fencer of the Twentieth Century" by the International Fencing Federation.

Le Champion olympique d'Escrime Christian D'ORIOLA et DUCASSE

Mathias, Bob—USA
Decathlon Gold

The Time magazine card depicts a magazine cover, and the text refers to the successful defence of his title in 1952.

WORLDWIDE SPONSOR 1988 OLYMPIC GAMES

The card aside has a printed signature.

Mimoun, Alain—France
10,000m Silver

He was defeated by Zatopek in 1948 and 1952 but won Gold in the marathon in 1956.

The postcard photo is from But & Club magazine, as is the d'Oriola card. Both are normally found as maximum cards for the first day of issue of the French 1953 sports set of stamps.

Alain MIMOUN, Champion de France d'Athlétisme

Ostermeyer, Micheline—France
Shot Put & Discus Gold
High Jump Bronze

Micheline Ostermeyer went on to carve herself a career as a concert pianist.

Card published by Time Out, 2011.

Papp, László—Hungary
Boxing—Middleweight—Gold

Black & white photo postcard, hand signed.

Patton, Mel—USA
200m, 4 x 100m Relay Gold

The card, published in 1988, depicts a Time magazine cover.

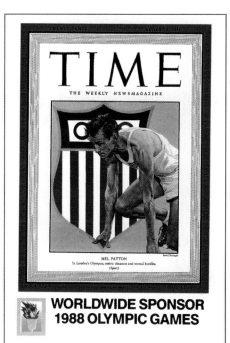

Van Vliet, Pietje ("Nelly") - Netherlands
Swimming—200m Breaststroke Gold

Both cards have printed signatures.

US Olympic Fencing Sabre Team
Bronze

The card was sent from Uxbridge (Olympic Village) by Miguel de Capriles. Other members of the team were Norman Armitage, George Worth, Tibor Nyilas, Dean Cetrulo, and James Flynn.

Women's Gymnastics Team
Czechoslovakia—Gold

The team names are printed on the reverse. The card illustrated is autographed by Vêra Rúžicková.

Olympiasieger 1948 - Turnen

Hungarian Olympic Champions

Face: A 1948 poster by Mátyás Gaál
Reverse: Gold medallists—
   Athletics: Olga Gyarmati (long jump)
         Imre Németh (hammer)
   Boxing: *Tibor Csik (bantam); László Papp (middlewt.)*
Gymnastics: *Ferenc Pataki (floor)*
Shooting: *Károly Takács (free pistol)*

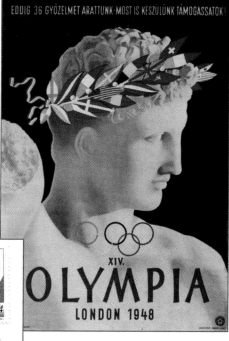

Wrestling: *Gyula Bóbis (super-heavywt)*
Fencing: *Ilona Elek (foil);*
         Aladár Gerevich (sabre)
      Sabre Team (Tibor Berezelly,
      Aladár Gerevich , Rudolf Kárpáti,
      László Rajesányi)

Post-1948 Postcards
British

*(See also Torch Relay and
Opening Ceremony chapter)*

DGA 107
Olympic Games—London
Poster 1948
Artist: Herz
Reproduced by kind permission of British Airways
Museum Collection

DRUMAHOE
GRAPHICS
POST CARD

National Postal Museum Olympic Exhibition
18p
18 Oct 1988
London EC1

Printed in Great Britain by Benc Tempest & Co Ltd St Ives Cornwall

MARY EVANS
PICTURE LIBRARY

T: +44 (0)20 8318 0034 pictures@maryevans.com

www.maryevans.com

Olympic Games souvenir programme, London 1948
Image 10057633 © Mary Evans Picture Library (2010)

"Rugby" Woodcut by John Platt exhibited London Olympiad 1948.
© Worldwide Langton Football Collection, London, England.

Winning Endeavours is a new website telling the story of London's sportsmen and women and their achievements during the twentieth century, including the 1908 and 1948 Olympic Games.

View hundreds of documents, personal accounts, posters, photographs and newspaper cuttings.

Features include: resource materials for schools and walk guides for exploring London's sporting heritage.

www.winningendeavours.org

This London 2012 print is the latest of many versions of the poster on a postcard (including the Olympic Museum (general), and Mars confectionery)

Reproduced from the original collection of the Olympic Museum, Lausanne.
Thank you for purchasing this Official Product of London 2012.
Your purchase supports the London 2012 Olympic and Paralympic Games.
Manufactured/Designed under license by The Art Group, a division of Pyramid International,
Pyramid Posters Limited, The Works, Park Road, Blaby, Leicester, LE8 4EF. Made in England
© 1948-2012 International Olympic Committee (IOC)   London 2012 Emblem © LOCOG 2007

31599

Canada Tire Change

Only the caption on the reverse indicates that this is an Olympic photo. There is no clue as to publisher, nor when or why the card was published.

1948 Olympics
Canada Tire Change

United States—Helms Bakeries
"Bread Flown to London's 1948 Olympic Games"

Helms issued a similar postcard after the 1932 Games in Los Angeles, and 1936 Berlin.

Torch Relay and Opening Ceremony
(see earlier chapter for additional cards)

Bicester, Oxfordshire, 2012

Coca Cola, Atlanta, 1996

Cigarette Cards
and other Collectors' Cards

A set of 50 cards was published by Carreras in Turf cigarettes. Because of the shortage of card the images and captions were printed on the slides themselves for packs of 10 or 20 cigarettes. Most of the cards are found cut out with scissors: straight edges and full margins are very much the exception. The full set is listed here. The captions show that they were printed shortly before the Games.

A selection of other collectors' cards is also shown, as examples. They range in date from about 1948 to more recent times.

Carreras 'Turf'

PETER BRANDER
(GREAT BRITAIN)
Outstanding lightweight amateur boxer in the country.
50 OLYMPICS 1948 Nº 1

HARRY CHURCHER
(GREAT BRITAIN)
Track walking champion who will compete in the 10000 metres walk.
50 OLYMPICS 1948 Nº 2

E. McDONALD BAILEY
(GREAT BRITAIN)
Native of Trinidad and the finest sprint runner outside the U.S.
50 OLYMPICS 1948 Nº 3

DON IRVINE
(GREAT BRITAIN)
A strongly fancied competitor in the free style wrestling.
50 OLYMPICS 1948 Nº 4

DENNIS SHORE
(SOUTH AFRICA)
Veteran track runner still breaking records from 100 to 400 metres.
50 OLYMPICS 1948 Nº 11

ANN CURTIS
(U.S.A.)
America's leading free style woman swimmer.
50 OLYMPICS 1948 Nº 5

ELINOR GORDON
(GREAT BRITAIN)
Young Scots girl who is 100 yards breast stroke swimming champion.
50 OLYMPICS 1948 Nº 6

MORRIS CUROTTA
(AUSTRALIA)
17 yeold quarter miler reckoned the best young prospect the Australians have.
50 OLYMPICS 1948 Nº 7

HERBERT McKENLEY
(JAMAICA)
World's record breaker at quarter mile and favourite for the Olympic 400 metres
50 OLYMPICS 1948 Nº 8

ROY ROMAIN
(GREAT BRITAIN)
This fifteen London Solicitor is the greatest breast stroke swimmer this country has ever had.
50 OLYMPICS 1948 Nº 9

CATHIE GIBSON
(GREAT BRITAIN)
Scots girl who is Britain's best woman swimmer.
50 OLYMPICS 1948 Nº 10

JOHN ARCHER
(GREAT BRITAIN)
The European 100 metres champion, and one of our sprint hopes for Wembley.
50 OLYMPICS 1948 Nº 12

ROY KERN
(GREAT BRITAIN)
Holder of the English springboard diving championship.
50 OLYMPICS 1948 Nº 13

J. RYAN
(GREAT BRITAIN)
Best known of all British amateur boxers, and a strong fancy for the welterweight title.
50 OLYMPICS 1948 Nº 14

M. WOOD
(AUSTRALIA)
A sculler who is expected to do well in the racing at Henley.
50 OLYMPICS 1948 Nº 15

REG. HARRIS
(GREAT BRITAIN)
Champion cyclist, and holder of the World's sprint title.
50 OLYMPICS 1948 Nº 16

ALAN BANNISTER
(GREAT BRITAIN)
Cycling team mate of Reg.Harris.Together they may form the tandem pair.
50 OLYMPICS 1948 Nº 17

JOHN B. KELLY
(U.S.A.)
World's best sculler and holder of the Henley Diamonds".
50 OLYMPICS 1948 Nº 18

JOHN MIKAELSSON
(SWEDEN)
One of the great Scandinavian walkers and former holder of the British miles title.
50 OLYMPICS 1948 Nº 19

W. ROBERTS
(GREAT BRITAIN)
400 metres runner and member of the British relay team who won in Berlin in 1936.
50 OLYMPICS 1948 Nº 20

JOHN TRELOAR
(AUSTRALIA)
His country's great sprinting discovery. Has done 9.5 for 100 yards.
50 OLYMPICS 1948 Nº 21

JACK WHITFORD
(GREAT BRITAIN)
The outstanding man gymnast in this country.
50 OLYMPICS 1948 Nº 22

C.T. WHITE
(GREAT BRITAIN)
British half mile champion and hope for the 1500 metres.
50 OLYMPICS 1948 Nº 23

LASSE HINDMAR
(SWEDEN)
In the first three of Sweden's great track walkers.
50 OLYMPICS 1948 Nº 24

MAUREEN GARDNER
(GREAT BRITAIN)
The greatest woman hurdler Britain has ever had.
50 OLYMPICS 1948 Nº 25

EDDIE CONWELL
(U.S.A.)
No 3 American sprinter, joint holder of the British 100 yards record.
50 OLYMPICS 1948 Nº 26

J. SEPHARIADES
(FRANCE)
His country's greatest sculler and a former winner of the Henley Diamonds.
50 OLYMPICS 1948 Nº 27

FRED OBERLANDER
(GREAT BRITAIN)
Heavyweight wrestling hope in the free style class.
50 OLYMPICS 1948 Nº 28

PETER KIPPAX
(GREAT BRITAIN)
The famous Burnley soccer player reckoned the finest amateur footballer in the country.
50 OLYMPICS 1948 Nº 29

J.S.JONES
(GREAT BRITAIN)
An international water polo star who has played many times for Britain.
50 OLYMPICS 1948 Nº 30

JACK WARDROP
(GREAT BRITAIN)
Product of the Motherwell School who will swim for Britain in the middle distance free style events.
50 OLYMPICS 1948 Nº 31

ELIZABETH CHURCH
(GREAT BRITAIN)
17 year old Northampton girl who is Britain's foremost breaststroke swimmer.
50 OLYMPICS 1948 Nº 32

JOHN WINTER
(AUSTRALIA)
Best high jumper his country has had for many years. Entirely self-taught, has cleared 6ft.7ins.
50 OLYMPICS 1948 Nº 34

JACK HALE
(GREAT BRITAIN)
Hull swimmer who specialises in the middle and long distance races.
50 OLYMPICS 1948 Nº 35

DEREK C. PUGH
(GREAT BRITAIN)
Second best in Europe over 400 metres.
50 OLYMPICS 1948 Nº 36

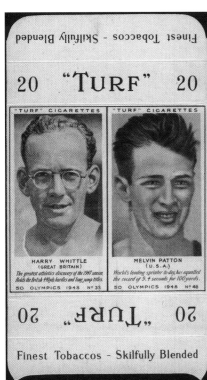

Index of Turf cards

1 Peter Brander	GB	Boxing	Featherweight	Lost first round
2 Harry Churcher	GB	Athletics	10km walk	5th
3 E. McDonald Bailey	GB	Athletics	100m	6th
4 Don Irvine	GB	Wrestling	Freestyle Welterweight	Did not compete
5 Ann Curtis	USA	Swimming	100m freestyle	Silver
			400m freestyle	Gold
			4 x 100m relay	Gold
6 Helen (Elinor) Gordon	GB	Swimming	200m breaststroke	Semi-final
7 Morris Curotta	Australia	Athletics	100m	Semi-final
			400m	5th
			4 x 100m relay	First round
8 Herbert McKenley	Jamaica	Athletics	200m	4th
		Athletics	400m	Silver
			4 x 400m relay	Final - did not finish
9 Roy Romain	GB	Swimming	200m breaststroke	Semi-final
10 Cathie Gibson	GB	Swimming	400m freestyle	Bronze
			100m backstroke	Semi-final
			4 x 100m relay	4th
11 Dennis Shore	South Africa	Athletics	200m	2nd round
			400m	Semi-final
12 John Archer	GB	Athletics	4 x 100m relay	Silver
13 Roy Kern	GB	Diving	Springboard	Did not compete
14 J Ryan	GB	Boxing	Welterweight	Did not compete
15 M Wood	Australia	Rowing	Single sculls	Gold
16 Reg. Harris	GB	Cycling	1000m scratch	Silver
			2000m tandem	Silver
17 Alan Bannister	GB	Cycling	2000m tandem	Silver
18 John B. Kelly	USA	Rowing	Single sculls	Semi-final
19 John Mikaelsson	Sweden	Athletics	10km walk	Gold
20 W Roberts	GB	Athletics	400m	2nd round
			4 x 400m relay	First round
21 John Treloar	Australia	Athletics	100m	Semi-final
			200m	Semi-final
			4 x 100m relay	First round
22 Jack Whitford	GB	Gymnastics		Did not compete
23 C. T. White	GB	Athletics	800m	Semi-final

24	Lasse Hindmar	Sweden	Athletics	Race walking	Did not compete
25	Maureen Gardner	GB	Athletics	80m hurdles	Silver
				4 x 100m relay	4th
26	Eddie Conwell	USA	Athletics		Did not compete
27	J. Sephariades	France	Rowing	Single sculls	Semi-final
28	Fred Oberlander	GB	Wrestling	Freestyle Heavyweight	Did not compete
29	Peter Kippax	GB	Football	(Soccer)	4th
30	J. S. Jones	GB	Water Polo		Not selected
31	Jack Wardrop	GB	Swimming	1500m freestyle	First round
32	Elizabeth Church	GB	Swimming	200m breaststroke	Semi-final
33	Harry Whittle	GB	Athletics	400m hurdles	Semi-final
				Long jump	7th
34	John Winter	Australia	Athletics	High jump	Gold
35	Jack Hale	GB	Swimming	400m freestyle	7th
				1500m freestyle	First round
				4 x 200m relay	First round
36	Derek C. Pugh	GB	Athletics	400m	2nd round
				4 x 400m relay	First round
37	Margaret Lucas	GB	Athletics		Did not compete
38	Harrison Dillard	USA	Athletics	100m	Gold
				4 x 100m relay	Gold
39	Margaret Walker	GB	Athletics	200m	5th
				4 x 100m relay	4th
40	J.C.M. Wilkinson	GB	Athletics		Did not compete
41	Donald Finlay	GB	Athletics	110m hurdles	First round
42	Jean Desforges	GB	Athletics		Did not compete
43	Prince A.F. Adedoyin	GB	Athletics	High Jump	12th
				Long jump	5th
44	Sylvia Cheeseman	GB	Athletics	200m	Semi-final
45	Marcel Hansenne	France	Athletics	800m	Bronze
				1500m	Final
46	Douglas Harris	New Zealand	Athletics	800m	Semi-final
47	Douglas Wilson	GB	Athletics	1500m	First round
48	Melvin Patton	USA	Athletics	100m	5th
				200m	Gold
				4 x 100m relay	Gold
49	H.J. Forbes	GB	Athletics	Race walking	Did not compete
50	J.T. Holden	GB	Athletics	Marathon	Did not finish

Kiddy's Favourites (Glasgow)

A set of 50 cards was published in 1948. Most, but not all, relate to 1948 competitors.

No. 1
Patsy Elsener (GB)
Diving—Silver & Bronze

No.6
Fritze Nathansen (DK)
Swimming—Silver

No. 9
Robert Wardrop (GB)
Swimming

No. 10
Henry Carpentier (*sic*)
should be Carpenter—
boxer (Flyweight)

No. 16
Elinor Gordon (*sic*)
should be Elenor
Swimming

No.35
H.G. Tarraway
Athletics

No. 47
Reg Harris
Cycling—2 silver

Other competitors depicted include:
2   Denis Shore (SA)—Athletics
3   John Treloar (AUS)—Athletics
5   Robert Forbes Gentleman (GB) — Water Polo
8   Jack Wardrop (GB)—swimming

Hollywood Series (France)

Lord Burghley

Card B8 in a series of 90 "Hollywood" brand cards published by La Pie Qui Chante in France in the 1930s (reproduced approximately actual size).

British Automatic Company— weighing machines

Cards from a series of 24 entitled "Speed", issued in 1949. Weighing machines could be found on many railway stations at the time.

2   J.F. Mikaelsson   Olympic 10,000m walk 1948
3   M.T. Wood   Olympic sculling champion 1948
4   F.E. Blankers-Koen Olympic 100 m record 1948
9   M. Ghella   Olympic cycling champion 1948

It is clear that other cards in the series will relate to 1948, but it is for collectors to discover if all are—they are not easy to find!

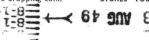

Comet Sweets

Cards from two series of cards (series of 25 and of 22) entitled "Olympic Achievements" (1960)

Plain grey back

Junior Service Sweet Cigarettes (1957)

Ken Jones won a Silver Medal in the 4 x 100m relay. He played rugby for Wales 1947-1957.

Brooke Bond (Tea Cards)

Olympic Greats (1979)

OLYMPIC GREATS

No.1
FANNY BLANKERS-KOEN
26.4.1918 —
HOLLAND
ATHLETICS
4 GOLD

A 30-year-old Dutch housewife, Fanny Blankers-Koen, outshone everyone at the 1948 Olympics held in London. By winning the 100 metres, 200 metres and 80 metres hurdles, and running the last leg for Holland's victorious relay team, the 'Flying Dutchwoman' became the first and only female athlete to gain four gold medals in the same Games.

Save all 40 cards in this series on a wallchart or in an album. You can obtain either by sending a 10p coin to Brooke Bond Oxo Ltd., Dept. OG, Parkway House, Sheen Lane, London SW14 8LU.

OLYMPIC GREATS

No.2
EMIL ZATOPEK
19.9.1922 —
CZECHOSLOVAKIA
ATHLETICS
4 GOLD; 1 SILVER

Known affectionately as the 'Bouncing Czech' or the 'Human Locomotive', Emil Zatopek was the superstar of the 1952 Olympics in Helsinki. In the space of a week, he easily won the 10,000 metres, captured the 5000 metres in a thrilling sprint finish, and finally romped away with the marathon in his first attempt at the distance! It remains an unique triple - and for good measure his wife Dana won the javelin.

Save all 40 cards in this series on a wallchart - or in an album. You can obtain either by sending a 10p coin to Brooke Bond Oxo Ltd . Dept. OG, Parkway House, Sheen Lane, London SW14 8LU

Olympic Challenge (1992)

OLYMPIC
challenge 1992

A Series of 40 Cards

3. FANNY BLANKERS-KOEN *(Hol)*

The first woman to return to top class Olympic competition after having a family, this remarkable 30-year-old Hollander became the first female athlete to gain four Gold medals at a single Olympics when she contested the 1948 Games in London. She won the 100 metres (11.9), 80 metres hurdles (11.2 Olympic record), 200 metres (24.4) and was involved in the 4x100 metres relay. Out of nine women's events, she won four and could have made it five if she had entered the long jump, as the winning distance was well below her world record of the time.

Photograph: Allsport

Special Album or Wallchart for your 40 Picture Cards: just send £1 (p&p) to Brooke Bond Foods Ltd (40p of which is helping to raise funds for the British Olympic Team) plus your name and address to: Picture Card Dept. OC, P.O. Box 100, Burnley, Lancs, BB11 1PG. UK residents only.

OLYMPIC
challenge 1992

A Series of 40 Cards

4. BOB MATHIAS *(USA)*

Teenage sensation of the 1948 London Olympics when, at 17, he won the decathlon, the tough régime of 10 athletic events in two days, having only taken to the sport less than six months earlier! He was the youngest winner of a men's athletics event in Olympic history. Decathlon events are (in order): 100 metres, long jump, shot putt, high jump, 400 metres, 110 metres hurdles, discus, pole vault, javelin and 1,500 metres. He secured a second Gold medal in Helsinki, 1952.

Photograph: Allsport

Special Album or Wallchart for your 40 Picture Cards: just send £1 (p&p) to Brooke Bond Foods Ltd (40p of which is helping to raise funds for the British Olympic Team) plus your name and address to: Picture Card Dept. OC, P.O. Box 100, Burnley, Lancs, BB11 1PG. UK residents only.

OLYMPIC
challenge 1992

A Series of 40 Cards

5. EMIL ZATOPEK *(Czech)*

Superstar of the 1952 Games in Helsinki, Finland. In a week, he won the unprecedented triple of 10,000 metres, 5,000 metres and, finally, romped home in the marathon ... on his first attempt at the 26.2 mile distance! All times (29-17, 14-06.6 and 2:23-03) were Olympic records. His wife, Dana, born on the same day as her husband in 1922, won the javelin within an hour of his closest victory, a 0.8 second win in the 5,000 metres, to make the Games a family triumph.

Special Album or Wallchart for your Cards: just send £1 (p&p) to [...] (40p of which is helping to rai [...] British Olympic Team) plus your [...] to: Picture Card Dept. OC, P [...] Burnley, Lancs, BB11 1PG. UK residents only.

Blue Band Margarine (Holland), 1954

John Mark lighting the Olympic cauldron.

Radio Fun

A set of 20 issued in 1956

No 14.   Reg Harris (2 cycling Silver)

British SPORTS STARS

A SERIES OF 20

14

REG HARRIS

Top-flight cyclist and five times World Sprint Champion, Reg Harris, now 36, started his cycling career at an early age. Was selected for World Championships in 1939 but temporarily lost his sight whilst engaged on military service with the Tank Corps. Won titles as an amateur up to 1949 when he turned professional. Within a year he had achieved the remarkable feat of winning the Professional World Championship as well. Reg Harris reckons to do 3,000 miles cycling training between Christmas and the spring.

PRESENTED WITH
RADIO FUN

REG HARRIS

Panini

A selection of the many stickers to be found

Colgate (Australia)

One of a series of cards issued on or with Colgate products in Australia at the time of the 1956 Melbourne Olympics.

Atlanta '96 Centennial Olympic Games Collection

63 Bob Richards—Pole Vault

69 Sport In Art Poster

Publisher Unknown (German?)

These cards have plain grey backs and appear to have come joined to other cards. The eight shown here relate to 1948. Details of other cards are not known.

Nostalgia Postcard Collectors' Club

Numerous series of cards were published in the 1990s. Three cards relate to the 1948 Olympics:

London Olympics, 1948
The Belgium runner, Gaston Reiff, winning the 5000m. Behind him is the Czech runner Emil Zatopek who from a position forty metres behind the leader began a spectacular sprint. His rigorous self-inflicted training had prepared him for long hours of relentless self-punishment and a capacity for sustained speed. A contemporary once said that Zatopek ran like a man who had just been stabbed in the heart, but his hunched, tortured style did not affect his speed. The crowd were on their feet as he dramatically closed the distance between himself and the leader; above the roar Reiff could hear the splashing of Zatopek just behind him; five yards more and Zatopek would undoubtedly have claimed gold.

This Edition © IRIS Publishing Ltd. MCMXC. Set 24   Photo © Hulton Picture Company

Preparations for the Olympics, March 1948
The 1948 Olympics in London were staged in post-war austerity, but despite this they were a great success. RAF stations at Uxbridge and West Drayton were prepared to accommodate 1,700 competitors and 800 officials. Here, blankets and mattresses were being carried into some of the cubicles which had been partitioned off to give competitors more privacy than the traditional barrack room layout. The buildings were improved and altered in preparation for the 1 July when the stations would be officially handed over to the Olympic Games authorities. The Air Ministry were happy to take this opportunity to upgrade the stations to a post-war standard.

This Edition © IRIS Publishing Ltd. MCMXCII. Set 42   Photo © Hulton Picture Company

Fanny Blankers-Koen, Olympics 1948
These Olympics were held amid post-war austerity, yet were considered successful. The most remarkable personality to emerge was thirty-year-old Dutch athlete Fanny Blankers-Koen. Although she arrived in London as the record holder in high jump and long jump, she didn't even compete in these events. Instead she carried off gold medals in four track events: 100 metres, 200 metres, 80 metres hurdles and 4 x 100 metres relay. She is seen here leaving the track after the third of her triumphs.

This Edition © IRIS Publishing Ltd. MCMXCII. Set 49   Photo © Hulton Picture Company

OH-XIV
A card in an Olympic Hosts series

OC-11
A card in an Opening Ceremony series

Vignettes—
Labels and Stickers, Decals, Matchbox Labels, Exhibition sheets

French Federation of Boxing

(DuBois 1)

Hungarian Olympic Committee

Icelandic Olympic Committee

Printed by Waterlow & Sons Ltd, London. Issued label in blue (perf.). Specimens with overprint and punch hole in brown (perf. and imperf.) (DuBois 5)

Polish Olympic Committee

Two fund-raising vignettes were issued, 10 zl in red on tan, and 20 zl in brown on tan or dark-blue on tan. Although not issued by the Polish Post Office, they were accepted for internal mail. There appears to be some size variation. (DuBois 2a, 2b, 2c)

Omega—Official Timing

This label seems to have been distributed around the world by the Swiss company—it is known on covers from Burma and Nyasaland.

United States Olympic Fund

The Dubois catalogue lists these large blue and red peelable decals (shown at approximately 50% life size) as probably issued for 1948. There are affinities with a 1936 Garmisch decal, though the use of "United States" indicates they are post 1940. Similar decals issued in 1955 or 1956 have text on the reverse specifically showing they were issued for those Games. No decals are reported as specifically relating to 1952.

(DuBois 12 & 13)

United States Olympic Fund

DuBois 3a—
pinkish-red

DuBois 3d—
reddish-purple

In 1939 the American Olympic Committee issued fund-raising vignettes for the planned 1940 St. Moritz and Helsinki Games, in four colours and showing a scene from the 1932 Los Angeles Olympic Games. In 1947 the design was re-used, with revised text "U.S. OLYMPICCOMMITTEE LONDON - 1948 GAMES—ST. MORITZ". There are inscriptions in the four margins. The top inscription (above) is as 1939 except that it is now headed "UNITED STATES VICTORY STAMP", and refers to the United States Olympic Committee (instead of 'American'). The bottom inscription is identical to the 1939. The left-side reads ".V OLYMPIC WINTER GAMES.ST.MORITZ, SWITZERLAND JANUARY 30—FEBRUARY 8, 1948". On the right: ".GAMES OF THE XIV OLYMPIAD.LONDON, ENGLAND. July 29-AUGUST 14, 1948."

The vignettes are engraved, and sheets are known imperf. A black, ungummed publicity proof, litho-printed is also known.

Marginal pair in green
as UK First Day Cover

Blue singles, used on
a cover to England

Matchbox Labels

Alsing, London (Made in Sweden)

There appear to be several printings of this label (rather than missing colours) (DuBois 6)

Solo A.G. Wien (Vienna)

Based on the same design as the matchboxes made for Alsing,

a)   *with '333' in the bottom right-hand corner* (DuBois 8)

b)   *without '333' in grey, green-blue and yellow* (DuBois 7)

'Olympia'

A number of labels can be found, in different sizes (32 x 45mm or 30 x 41mm) with 'OLYMPIA' at the top and 'SOLO B.F.I.' or 'SOLO K.S.I.' or just ' B.F.I.' at the foot. These are generally considered to have been produced in 1948, but Ernest Trory suggests they were issued in 1936. Germany's Heiko Volk lists them as 1948.

(DuBois 9, 10, & 11)

'FIVE RINGS'

This box and the matches were made in Japan, but the Japanese were excluded from the 1948 Games. (Dubois 14)

MSZ—Olympic Champions

A set of labels, believed to be Dutch, including 69—Fanny Blankers-Koen, 71—Bob Mathias, 72—Wilbur Thompson (USA) Shot Put

Exhibition Sheets

Stampex, London 1962

The exhibition souvenir sheet featured stamp reproductions in black, including Abram Games 3^d Olympic stamp.

North West Showpex, Manchester, 1980

The sheet reproduces all four Olympic values in colour.

Stampex, London, 1984

The exhibition sheet (which came in a Stampex 1984 folder) celebrated the Los Angeles Olympics of that year and depicted two unissued Olympic stamps (from Australia and Germany) and the 1948 2½^d stamp tied with a printed pseudo-cancel. The sheet can also be found in a glossy black.

Scarborough Philatelic Society

One of a series of 'spoof' sheetlets substituting the head of King Edward VIII for that of George VI (text refers to '2 stamps' in error).

Gold Stamps

The source and origin of these labels is unclear.

Esso Collectors' Labels

These are peelable labels given away in packs at petrol stations, size 153 x 97mm they have one, two or three images. The smaller labels relating to 1948 come se-tenant with other labels. All were intended to be stuck into a book "The Olympics 1896-1972" published by Esso Petroleum Company Ltd in support of the British Olympic Appeal, and sold for just 25p.

No 15   1948 poster

No 16   Harrison Dillard
        (Gold 100m and 4 x 100m relay)

No 17   Bob Mathias (Gold, decathlon)

No 18   Fanny Blankers-Koen (4 Gold medals)

No 19   Tapio Rautavaara (Gold, javelin)
also
No 20   Emil Zatopek (1952)

General Ephemera

This chapter outlines paper collectibles under various generic headings. There is an enormous range and variety of material. The headings are indicative, and listings representative; one of the pleasures of collecting ephemera is that there is always something new to discover. Some ephemera is illustrated in the Torch Relay chapter.

Information Sheet—Programme

This information is not set out in the Official Report. Note that weightlifting and wrestling actually took place at Empress Hall, Earls Court, as did gymnastics because the pitch at the Stadium was waterlogged.

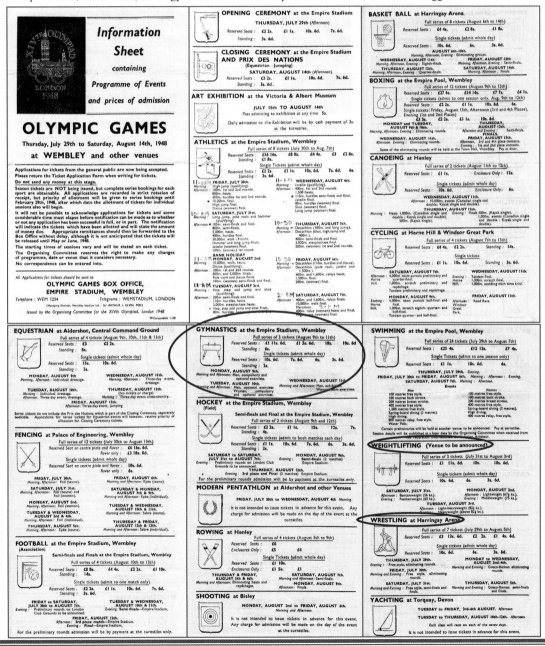

Report to the International Olympic Committee

The Report
OF THE
CHAIRMAN OF THE ORGANISING COMMITTEE
FOR THE
XIV Olympiad London 1948
TO THE
INTERNATIONAL OLYMPIC COMMITTEE

A 16 page report (135 x 215mm) made in September 1946 by Lord Burghley, in English and French, no doubt one of a series of reports.

Official Handbook of Information

XIV OLYMPIAD
LONDON 1948

OFFICIAL HANDBOOK
of
INFORMATION

MANUEL OFFICIEL
de
RENSEIGNEMENTS

MANUAL OFICIAL
de
INFORMACION

Issued by the Organising Committee to
CHEFS DE MISSION, TEAM MANAGERS and OFFICIALS
Publié par le Comité Organisateur à l'intention des
CHEFS DE MISSION, des DIRECTEURS D'EQUIPE et des
PERSONNALITES OFFICIELLES
Publicado por el Comité Organizador para uso de los
JEFES DE MISION, DIRECTORES DE EQUIPOS y
MIEMBROS OFICIALES

The official Handbook for Chefs de Mission, Team Managers and Officials, in English, French and Spanish

XIV OLYMPIAD
LONDON 1948

GENERAL

REGULATIONS AND

PROGRAMME

THE ORGANISING COMM
THE XIV OLYMPIAD · LON

Regulations

These documents were published in English, French and Spanish, for each sport, and supplied to Olympic Committees and sports bodies around the world.

XIV OLYMPIADE
LONDRES 1948

ATHLETISME

XIV OLIMPÍADA
LONDRES 1948

MANUAL
DE
TIRO

COMITÉ ORGANIZADOR DE LA
XIV OLIMPÍADA · LONDRES 1948

XIV OLYMPIAD
LONDON 1948

YACHTING

THE ORGANISING COMMITTEE FOR
THE XIV OLYMPIAD LONDON 1948

Newsletters

Quarto-sized pages stapled together, in English, French, or Spanish (paper stock varies). Note change of address between January and March 1948.

There were at least 11 issues (the last seen is dated June 1948).

Organising Committee Correspondence

The letter of 15th July (below right) is 8" x 10" (221 x 254mm) on cream paper watermarked 'Adelphi Writings'. Another is known on 'Hylton Bond' watermarked paper. The letter-head is flat litho printed, and the signature is applied in pale-blue (not personally signed). There is no address, suggesting the paper stock was printed about the time the Organising Committee were moving.

The letter of 12th August 1948 (which came in its original envelope—see the Torch Relay chapter) is on paler cream paper with 'ABERMILL BOND MADE IN GT BRITAIN' watermark, and rich raised text and rings in the letter-head.

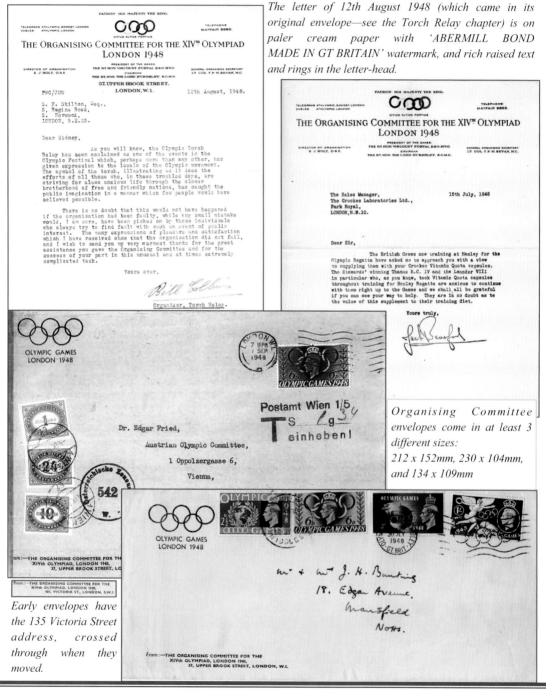

Organising Committee envelopes come in at least 3 different sizes: 212 x 152mm, 230 x 104mm, and 134 x 109mm

Early envelopes have the 135 Victoria Street address, crossed through when they moved.

Correspondence to the Organising Committee

Covers may be found from time to time. They cast light on Olympic postal history from around the world in 1948.

The Egyptian Olympic Committee

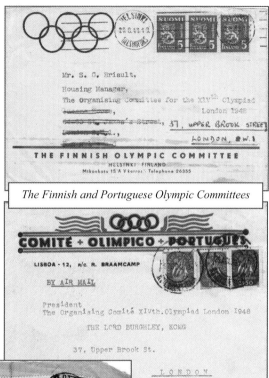

The Finnish and Portuguese Olympic Committees

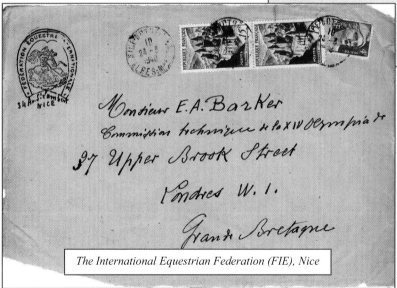

The International Equestrian Federation (FIE), Nice

Olympic Information Sheet

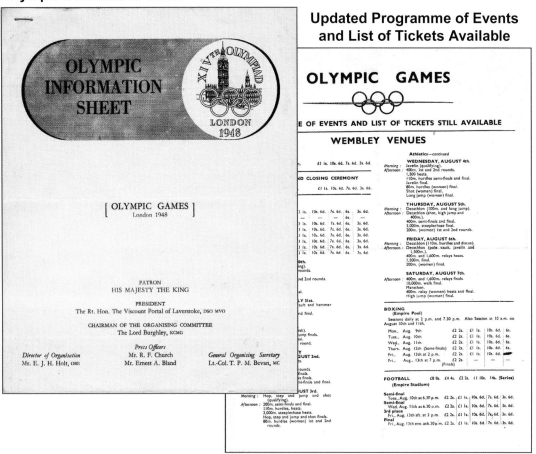

Updated Programme of Events and List of Tickets Available

Overseas Guides and Handbooks

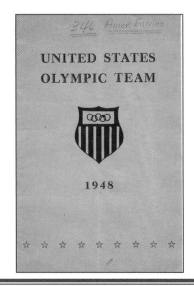

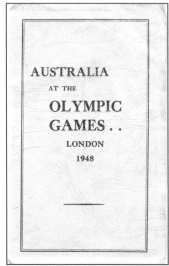

Poland

Maps

*The **London Transport** map is the most commonly found. It has a scale plan of Wembley on one side, and a schematic map in blue, with all the underground lines in white on the reverse.*

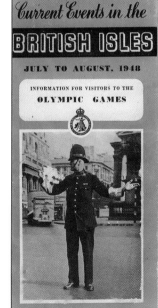

Other maps are much less common.

Current Events in the British Isles

KLM Map

Guides & Souvenir Brochures

Official Souvenir (A4 approx)

180 pages; Olympic history; events etc.

a.   *American Edition has dollar price*

b.   *Hardback edition has oversize linen-bound cover with gold embossed text.*

THE OLYMPIC GAMES OFFICIAL SOUVENIR

ADPRINT LIMITED
*APPOINTED OFFICIAL PRODUCERS BY THE ORGANISING
COMMITTEE OF THE OLYMPIC GAMES LONDON 1948
PUBLISHED AND DISTRIBUTED BY FUTURA PUBLICATIONS LTD*

51ᴀ RATHBONE PLACE LONDON W.I
TELEPHONE : MUSEUM 7788 (15 Lines)
TELEGRAMS : ADPRINT WESDO LONDON

IT IS REQUESTED THAT NO REFERENCE OR REVIEW APPEARS BEFORE JUNE 22ND

We have pleasure in enclosing herewith a review copy of the
Olympic Games Official Souvenir, to be published on the 22nd June
at 5s. net (£1. in the Western Hemisphere).   A press conference
will be held in these offices at 3.0 p.m. on June 15th when any
additional information you may require can be supplied, but would
you please let us know whether you wish to attend.

This Souvenir, the only official one to be authorised by the
Organising Committee of the Olympic Games, London 1948, has been
designed for international circulation as a worthy memento of a
great occasion, both for those who will see the Games and for the
many who will be unable to do so.

The production and distribution of 290,000 copies to a
strict time-table has been a printing and publishing achievement
of some magnitude.   Its world-wide coverage is in fact quite
unique for a British publication of any type.

Over half the total of 290,000 copies has been dispatched
for sale in North and South America, and all countries
participating in the Games will receive supplies.

Copies will be on sale in Great Britain from the 22nd June
at all leading newsagents and bookshops.

The publication has been produced by Adprint Ltd. and
published by the proprietors of FUTURE MAGAZINE.

*Cover of hardback edition (above), and Gymnastic
Souvenir with a similar cover*

Civic Guides

High Wycombe & District *Olympic Entertainment Committee presented a brochure on High Wycombe to the rowing and canoeing competitors. A4-sized, it has a stiff textured card cover and is cord bound.*

(They also presented a souvenir postcard of the Henley course (see the postcard chapter)).

Henley-on-Thames Souvenir Guide

A 52-page booklet c. 120 x 180mm produced by the Henley-on-Thames and District Chamber of Trade. It was on sale to the public, price 1/-. The Chamber would not pay £250 asked to permit the Olympic Rings to be printed on the cover.

Wembley Journal

A civic monthly, 24 pages plus cover, the August 1948 issue being devoted to the Games.

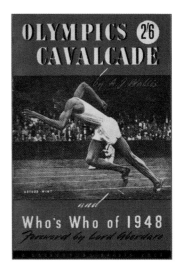

The London Olympic Games
pub. S. Evelyn Thomas
96pp. c. 138 x 215mm

Olympiad 1948
H.J. Oaten pub. Findon
116pp. c. 143 x 215mm

Olympics Cavalcade
A.J. Wallis
pub. Background Sports

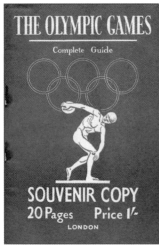

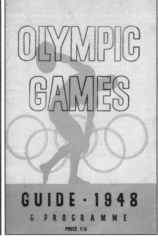

**The Olympic Games
Complete Guide**
20pp 1/-

Olympic Games Guide 1948
Court & Ross pub. Gloucester Press
56pp. c. 125 x 185mm

**Olympic Games
Souvenir**
*published by
Athletics Pictorial*

*The Illustrated
London News is
an invaluable
source of pre-
Olympic reports
and photographs
(as well as
Games reports)*

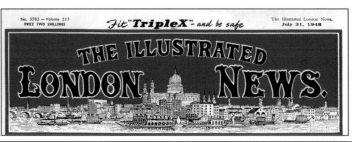

Pre-Games Publication Supplements or Special Issues

World Sports

The official magazine of the British Olympic Association had Olympic features throughout 1948. The July 1948 edition was the principal pre-Olympic edition. (August and September featured results and reports).

There were numerous other publications in Britain and around the world; those illustrated here are examples of the variety of publications to be found.

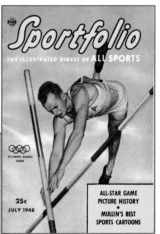

Daily Telegraph Guide to the Olympic Games and London
(Daily Telegraph Map and Guide of London)

32 pages of maps with the Olympic programme and supporting information, plus a large coloured folded map of the London area, and out to show the more distant venues.. The location maps supplement information in the Official Report.

After the Games, remaining stocks had two stickers placed on the front, renaming the brochure as "Map and Guide of London" and stating "Specially prepared for the recent Olympic Games, this is one of the finest Guides to London available."

Silshine Children's Toy Transfers

A booklet 95 x 137mm containing two sheets (4 panes) of children's skin transfers depicting various sports. The text on the transfers is inverted.

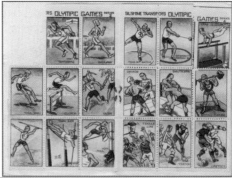

Tickets

Tickets were generally sent out in an envelope with an Olympic franking machine impression (meter) and covering letter:

Series Tickets

Series Tickets were despatched in a small folder with a window showing the sport or venue on the tickets within:

Tickets were printed with a stub at the left (retained by the Ticket Office), the main ticket to be retained by the spectator, and one or more counterfoils at the right, to be handed in on entry. Tickets found with all parts intact will never have been issued.

Tickets came in many colours. All had common text on the back. This prohibited filming, but not the taking of photographs.

As well as standard tickets for the public, there were tickets for competitors, the press etc. Tickets and invitations for special events did not follow the standard format but were individually designed. Staff and other passes giving access to venues etc., but not seats, are generally similar to what we would call credit-card sized today.

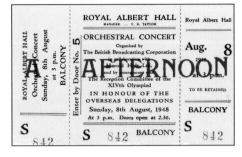

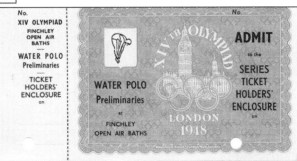

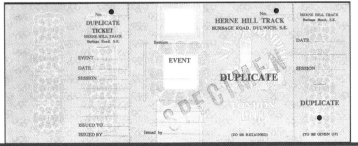

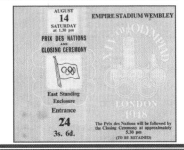

Programmes

Daily event programmes are in a standard format, but with different coloured front covers for each day for each sport. The Opening Ceremony programme is a larger publication, and there are unofficial Opening Ceremony programmes. Programmes for events other than the main sports vary in size and content.

Wembley Stadium Programme

A simple card folder c. 145 x 220 mm listing the Opening Ceremony, athletic, and gymnastic events in the Stadium [the latter moved to Empress Hall, Earl's Court], and also the swimming event in the Empire Pool.

Programme for officials and athletes

Preliminary Events and Trials

*Programmes for selection events, trials and preparatory or warm-up events, in Britain and other countries, are much more difficult to find than Olympic event programmes, and much more varied in style. The **British Amateur Wrestling Championships** programme is particularly rare. **1948 U.S. Olympic Team Trial** programmes can be found more easily. All have the same illustration on the front cover, and, usually, but not always, details of the specific trial.*

Olympic Yachting Torquay

Programmes for the Opening and Closing Ceremonies

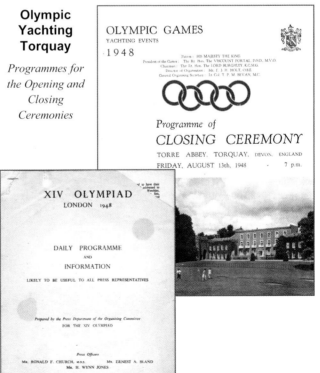

Daily Programme and Information Likely to be Useful to all Press Representatives

These consist of stapled pages.

Photographs

*Photos are available to collect originating from all the regular agencies and principal newspapers from around the world, many of them wire photos. There are photos of informal moments as well as sporting events and achievements. They are in general beyond the scope of this book, but mention must be made of the **Olympic Photo Association**, set up exclusively to provide photographs of the Games, and their collectable, but rarely surviving, envelopes.*

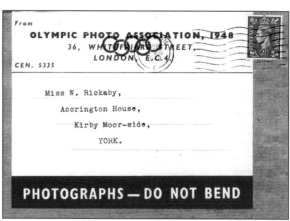

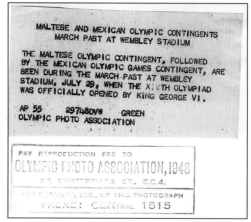

Postcard-sized photos:
London Transport Olympic Buses

B. E. Webb Photos

Three different cards are known. Contemporaneous or early prints can be found, but there are also modern reprints.

A large variety of photos were taken by Webb, and apparently commercialised from his premises in Leigh-on-Sea

Miscellaneous
Beer mats

Both contemporary and later beer mats can be found, from Great Britain and other countries. It is often hard to tell the year of origin.

Competitor's Ration Coupon

With food rationing in place, competitors were given extra coupons, for essentials and for treats!

The Railway Executive and London Transport Executive Travel Pass

A small embossed linen-bound folder with a pull-out travel map

XIVth OLYMPIAD 19704
CHOCOLATE AND CONFECTIONERY RATION

4 OUNCES

AVAILABLE UP TO...........

Notepaper from the British Olympic Mess, Salamanca Barracks, Aldershot. This may or may not be contemporary

BBC Broadcasting Handbook

Also, the BBC Yearbook for 1949 includes a feature article on broadcasting the Olympic Games.

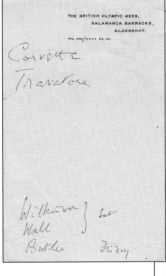

THE BRITISH OLYMPIC MESS,
SALAMANCA BARRACKS,
ALDERSHOT.

Luggage Label

Children's comics had inspiring Olympic articles and features.

READ ABOUT **THE 1936 OLYMPIC STARS**

THE ROVER

Reports and post-Games publications
Official Reports

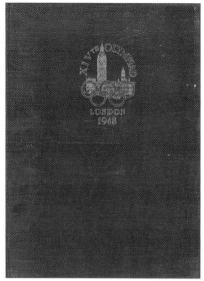

The Official Report of the Organising Committee for the XIV Olympiad, was published in 1951 (580pp, hardback, linen bound). Before that, **World Sports** published the *Official Report of the British Olympic Association* (112pp paperback). Olympic organisations around the world published reports reflecting national performances. These can be an invaluable source of photographs, biographies etc.

Olympiaden 1948

An example of a pictorial report, in this instance from Denmark.

Official Result of Events

A card folder 265 x 210mm, Torch-lighting on the front, release of doves on the back.

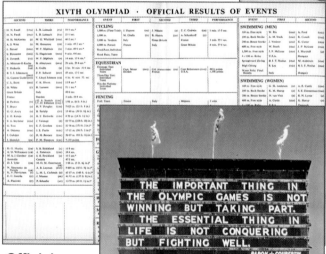

USA 1948 (Heinz Photo Co)
Ring-bound, perspex covered card pages of photos, mostly of the US team.

XIV Olympic Games
1948 Results & Records

Published in Australia by the Olympic Tyre & Rubber Co Ltd, a company founded by 1908 Olympic Silver medallist Frank Beaurepaire who came to London in 1948 to lobby for Melbourne's bid for the 1956 Games.

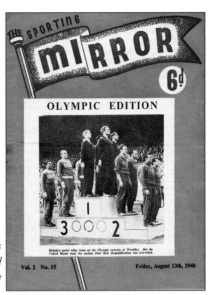

Sporting Mirror

One of very many publications giving Games results and reports, whether for the whole Games, or individual sports.

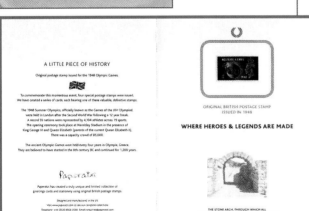

Lancaster's Salute to Barney Ewell

An example of a tribute event programme: for an athletics meeting shortly after the Games, paying tribute to one of the Gold Medal winning 4 x 100m relay team, who went to Lancaster High School (Pennsylvania). (He also won Silver in the 100m and 400m)

We close this overview of 1948 Olympic ephemera with a greetings card from 2012 that has an original 1948 stamp on the front (there is a set of four). All the other ephemera illustrated is from around 1948. This card just demonstrates that there will always be something new for the collector!

Acknowledgements, Sources and Bibliography

Douglas Muir, Curator Philately, British Postal Museum and Archive

The Philatelic Bulletin, February, March & April 1989

British Postal Museum and Archive

Post 52/1002 Unified Stamps - Olympic Games, issue and airletter

Post 102/12 Commemorative stamp issues, Channel Islands, Olympic Games and U K regional issues

James Mackay

British Postmark Bulletin: *Volume 31 Nos 2 & 3, 2001: Wembley and its Postmarks*

                                          Volume 34 Nos 5, 6 & 8: Olympic Postmarks

Postmarks of England and Wales (ISBN 09064400467)

Skeleton Postmarks of England & Wales, 3rd Edition compiled by Patrick G. Awcock and John R. Frost 2006 (ISBN 0900214120)

W. G. Stitt Dibden

The 1948 Olympics at Wembley (1959) (Reprinted in "Wembley & Olympic Issues, The Stamps & associated Postal Markings" published by the Postal History Society and the G.B. Philatelic Society)

Mark C. Maestrone & Joan R Bleakley

Olympians on Stamps 1896-1994 published by *Sports Philatelists International*

Alvaro Trucchi

I Vincitori di Medaglie Olimpiche published by *Unione Italiana Collezionisti Olimpici e Sportivi (UICOS)*

Jose M.ª Vidal Torrens, Guiseppe Sabilli Fioretti & Jose M.ª Soler Vila

Post, Philately and Olympism published by the International Olympic Committee 1986

Naomi Games

Arthur Reeder, Isle of Wight Postal Museum, Newport, Isle of Wight   www.postalmuseum.co.uk

Stamp Catalogues—

Stanley Gibbons Stamps of the World; Great Britain Concise; My Collection Online
Scott Postage Stamp Catalogue (as cited in Olympians on Stamps),
Michel Briefmarken Katalog, (for stamps of uncertain status not listed in other catalogues)
Catalogue Olympique 1896-1996 published by Yvert & Tellier (ISBN 2-86814-073-4)

Individual collectors:

Alan Sabey, Manfred Bergman, Michael Berry, Jean-Pierre Caravan, John Crowther, Steffen Eckstein, Bob Farley, Barrie King, Josef Koči, the late Vic Manikian, Mike Pagomenos, Jonathan Rosenthall, Manfred Winternheimer

Sources of information and philatelic items:

Adrian Bradbury, BFDC Ltd, www.bfdc.co.uk   Tony Bray   www.tonybray.co.uk
www.delcampe.net   www.eBay.co.uk
www.eBid.net   Heiko Volk   www.olympiaphilatelie-volk.de

The British Library and British Newspaper Library   www.bl.uk

The Official Report of the Organising Committee for the XIV Olympiad, 1951

     (see also www.la84foundation.org/6oic/OfficialReports/1948/OR1948.pdf)

THE SOCIETY OF OLYMPIC COLLECTORS

The Society of Olympic Collectors was founded in 1984, as a philatelic society, and remains the only English language philatelic society specialising exclusively in the Olympic theme.

The Society is recognised as a member of the Olympic Family by the International Olympic Committee, and has signed an agreement with the London Organising Committee for the Olympic Games 2012 (LOCOG) recognising its status as a society for collectors and its role in recording the postal history and collectables of the Olympic Games.

Torch Bearer

Our forty eight page colour journal is issued four times a year, offering news, articles and regular check-lists of Olympic material world-wide, not just postally related or philatelic, but including memorabilia, postcards 'Official' or 'Sponsor' produced souvenirs, and other collectables.

Articles deal with past and future celebrations of the Olympic Summer and Winter Games, as well as material related to the structure of the modern Olympic movement. Thanks to the efforts of our members, and our links within the Olympic movement and with our sister societies world-wide, Torch Bearer is an up-to-date and informative journal, essential reading for Olympic collectors.

There are opportunities to share your views, and news, through 'Members Forum' and 'News from Members' and to submit articles.

Society Auction

Our postal Auction List is distributed with each issue of Torch Bearer and offers the opportunity to sell and buy material amongst collectors with a common interest. The auction enjoys a high level of sales and presents a regular chance to add to your collection.

E-mail Newsletter

Our e-newsletter enables members to receive the latest news very quickly.

International Packet

All members may participate in the International Circulating Packet. Original Olympic and sports stamps and postal history items are sent to the Packet Manager together with photocopies or scans. The Manager circulates the copies, not the material itself, so there are no insurance problems compared with a traditional packet.

All items are offered at fixed prices, and a good level of sales is achieved!

Society Library

The Society Library is available as a resource to all members.

Publications and Souvenirs

The Society has produced a number of handbooks for collectors, and will continue to do so: Beijing 2008 and London 2012 are being, and will continue to be well documented by SOC!

The Society produces a modest number of philatelic and postal souvenirs each year, including London 2012 Olympic and Paralympic items exclusive to members.

Membership of the Society of Olympic Collectors

Membership is by CALENDAR year. All back issues of Torch Bearer for the current year will be sent to members joining during the year. Renewals become due on 1st January irrespective of the date of joining and may be paid in multiples. For Junior Members aged under 18 year subscription rates are half of the adult rate.

Annual Subscription Rates for 2012 are £14 p.a. (UK), £17 p.a. (Europe), £19 p.a. (World) (PayPal is accepted) For further details, including subscription rates for 2013-2016, and a membership application form please e-mail
secretary@societyofolympiccollectors.org *or*
visit our developing web-site www.societyofolympiccollectors.org

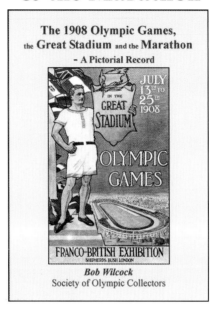